love you
libra

Also by Howard Cunnell

The Sea on Fire

Marine Boy

HOWARD CUNNELL

Fathers & Sons

PICADOR

First published 2017 by Picador
an imprint of Pan Macmillan
20 New Wharf Road, London N1 9RR
Associated companies throughout the world
www.panmacmillan.com

ISBN 978-1-5098-1216-5

The Acknowledgements on pp. 211–13 constitute an extension of this copyright page.

1 3 5 7 9 8 6 4 2

A CIP catalogue record for this book is available from the British Library.

Printed and bound by CPI Group (UK) Ltd, Croydon, CR0 4YY

Visit **www.picador.com** to read more about all our books
and to buy them. You will also find features, author interviews and
news of any author events, and you can sign up for e-newsletters
so that you're always first to hear about our new releases.

For Paul

Often I am permitted to return to a meadow
as if it were a scene made-up by the mind,
that is not mine, but is a made place,
that is mine, it is so near to the heart

Robert Duncan,
Often I Am Permitted to Return to a Meadow

Brixton, London, 2003

Jay is running.

Her long brown hair ribbons out behind her. Che and Krystian try to win the ball, but my daughter keeps it under control as the boys attack her from both sides. Jay bursts through a space between them and shoots low and hard. The ball makes a fast scraping sound as it travels over concrete and through dry leaves into the makeshift goal.

She's seven. What's she thinking as she runs so fast? Does she notice the familiar high-sided building enclosing her – the blurred iron railings and walkways and arches of the flats that look onto the yard and seem to move as she moves – or does the certainty of her home, its always being there, permit her not to see or think about it, but to be held in an understanding of its permanence in such a way that she is untroubled? Secure. Free. I hope so, it's what I want for her.

Cardinal points are always there, they don't change. You don't have to think about them until you're lost.

In autumn sunshine – tawny, soft, faintly edged with cold – cats sleep on the walkways, dappled paws and legs and tails poking out and twitching between the railings.

I need to tell Jay that I'm not her blood father.

I want her to have a little more time not knowing everything, before I take certainty away for ever. This was the world, Jay, now it's changed. I'm scared that if I take away her dad a black hole will take the place in her heart where her love for me is growing now.

That's what can happen when you don't know who you are. If you let it, your life's story becomes about what isn't there, not what is. I have to make a new story – really, it's urgent now. I can't wait any longer to tell Jay.

She runs in sunshine, close to where I stand watching, Che and Krystian on her heels. The boys love her but it's complicated. She's a mate, one of the gang, the best at football though Krys won't admit this. She can run the fastest, beat them at any game, but she's a girl, with long hair falling past her waist, and a flawless, heart-shaped brown face and bright red lips. The boys love her, even as she races past and beats them again. My strong and light-footed daughter is full of grace.

Sometimes Che and Krystian have to have boy talks and they exclude her, or meet secretly. When that happens Jay sits alone at the top of the little fort in the communal garden and plays on her Game Boy. She doesn't want to be different to them and doesn't think she is, but the boys feel a difference. There are things they won't do or can't say in front of her.

I wonder about this. How she outboys the boys. If she was a boy she'd be the leader, but when Krys – a long-haired, stocky Polish boy who's a head shorter than Jay – comes to call for her, you can see by his mooncalf gaze how her beauty blasts and disturbs him. I don't think he can quite understand how he's supposed to feel.

Our ground-floor front door opens to an arch straight onto the communal garden. I stand under the arch that is always in shadow and watch Jay run. I could watch for ever but it's time for Jay to come in and have a bath with her little sister, Rose.

I leap out and grab her around the waist and pick her up and swing her. She screams happily. She loves to fight me. She likes to see how strong she is – to test herself and test me. I know she thinks that every time we fight is a time closer to when she'll be able to beat me. She's so good to hold and look at.

She struggles to get free and I hold her closer. I breathe in her young animal smell. I kiss her neck and blow a raspberry through her hair and against her warm skin.

Arggh! Get off me Dad!

She's strong, all long, hard muscled legs and wiry arms. It's all I can do to hold her to me. She wants to get back to Che and Krys and the game.

I hold her tighter and she pretends to bite me, snapping her teeth at me and being a zombie.

She's panting.

Hold still Jay.

She has drawings all up her arms. Dolphins and daggers (there are dolphins on her T-shirt, too). Her jeans pockets are stuffed with Pokemon cards.

If I don't do it now it'll be full of knots later – then it'll be ten times as bad.

Lemme go Dad!

I pick her up and turn her upside down. A Pikachu card

falls from her pocket. She screams and grabs for it but I hold her higher so she can't reach. Her hair falls in a shining cascade to the ground. I pretend to beat her with the plastic back of the hairbrush. I turn her the right way up. Hair covers her face and she's laughing all the time. She parts the curtain of hair and sticks her tongue out at me, shrieks and closes the curtain.

She stands in front of me all hunched up, her arms raised in a monster pose, panting and laughing at the same time.

Come on Bear Bum, I say, I really need to do this now.

Something in my voice makes her snap to attention.

Sir! Yessir! she says.

She stands straight as a knife, arms by her side. She's trying to keep a straight face.

I put one hand on her chest to keep her still. Her heart is thumping. The fingers of my other hand harrow through her hair, looking for the worst of the knots. When I find them, I gently try to untangle them with my fingers and then brush the hair.

Jay tries not to cry out when I find a knot. When her mother does this, Jay screams the place down. With me she's trying to be a good soldier. More than this, she knows the boys pretending not to watch will tease her if she makes a fuss.

She pushes her body out until it makes a bow.

She makes animal shapes with her fingers, and then reaches back to attack me.

OK stand still Bear.

I begin to brush Jay's hair. From the top of her head, I

push the brush all the way down to past her waist. Static electricity makes her hair start to frizz out, and wild filaments are softly illuminated by the last of the sunshine. She's quiet now, tracing on the arm that holds her the patterns of my tattoos. I'm humming as I pass the brush through her hair over and over.

She's a kid. She's used to being acted upon, to having her life paused and controlled. I hope and feel she's being soothed by her dad brushing her hair, but mostly she is waiting to be released.

I think of Gary Snyder's poem 'Axe Handles'. Snyder teaching his son, Kai, how to shape wood into an axe handle. Look, the poet says to the boy, we'll shape the handle by checking the handle of the axe we cut with. Snyder remembers the Chinese saying, centuries old: when making an axe handle the pattern is not far off.

Shaped and shaper, what kind of axe am I?

Che and Krystian carry on playing but their hearts aren't in it. They're arguing about whose turn it is to go in goal. They need their Jay back, especially Krys.

Carefully, I separate Jay's hair into three thick and roughly equal parts. I place one strand over each narrow shoulder. The central strand hangs down her back. It's too thin, and I borrow hair from the outside until I'm satisfied the parts are equal in thickness. I start brushing again and Jay sighs and kind of softly deflates.

Hang on, I say, won't be long now.

Jay slowly raises her left leg and holds it raised, lifts her arms, holds them raised, her hands joined together and pointing downwards. She makes a squawking noise.

A crane? I say, braiding her hair, pulling the braids tight against one another.

Hah, she says quietly, good Dadda.

She puffs out her cheeks. Sticks her belly out. Makes little ears out of her closed fists and puts them by the side of her head. She growls.

A bear?

Course, she says.

It's now – her young heart beating hard against my hand – that Jay, beyond everything else she is, feels most strongly like a gift.

What comes to me as I stand brushing Jay's hair is that because there is no shared blood, the strength or otherwise of the connection between us will always rely on love and love only. The love I show to Jay and her two sisters and to their mother will always come back to me amplified.

Love is the shaping axe.

Eastbourne, East Sussex, 1970

To the beach, through a galaxy of daytime stars.

Mum, darkly suntanned, wears a white cheesecloth blouse and a pale denim skirt. She's still in her early twenties but her slight, boyish body makes her look even younger. She could be our sister. Luke and I wear sunshine-clean T shirts, shorts and sandals. I'm five or six. Luke's three years older than me. Summer brings out the redness in our hair. A chestnut wave falls past Mum's shoulders. My hair is copper, like a new penny. Luke has a headful of fire.

The rising sun hits the houses we walk by, and windows are no longer three-dimensional objects solidly contained within straight frames, but starbursts of uncontained light.

Early morning in Eastbourne, on the south coast. We've been in Sussex for generations, labourers working on the land or women in service. Mum's dad was a soldier. Mum broke away when she was sixteen but now she's back, with two young boys.

It's a conservative town. People are quick to judge. Mum is always neat. Chic – this is her life now, before it's really started, but she's read Russian novels and seen Sammy Davis dance at the Talk of the Town. We are clean, polite, well-turned-out boys, but in this town, people who don't know you think they can interfere.

—

To get to the beach from Churchdale Place – the closed-off street where we live – you turn left on to Churchdale Road and walk south. If you turn right you soon come to undeveloped land – waste ground – where I dig hideouts and hunt for olive grass snakes. Mostly I'm alone, sometimes with Luke – who keeps his grass snakes in cardboard boxes in our room. At least he did once, I'm sure, though Luke might not remember. The same way I remember a terrified bird, caked with soot so that you could not tell what kind of bird it was, flying into our room from the disused chimney (how did it get caught in there, and fall, a bird?), black soot showering from its beating wings as it tried to escape, and Luke doesn't. I don't remember that, he'll say, or, you've got that wrong, that's not what happened. Black marks on the walls and floor. Mum finally getting the bird out the open window.

A small caravan of clouds drifts south, underlit by the rising sun.

Does Luke see the novas of light that were once windows in the houses we walk past on our way to the beach? My brother walks ahead. He's protecting us. In the winter we watched *The Last of the Mohicans* and Luke is being Chingachgook, stepping noiselessly and without fear through the forest.

Beyond the open space of wildflowers and dumped rubbish are railway tracks. At night I listen to the trains going away to London, the fabulous city where Mum lived with Dad and Luke until Dad left and Mum had to come back. I listen to the fading click-clack of the last train and think about my father. In the dark I lie awake in clean sheets, as the sound of the going-away train fades to silence, terrified by how badly somebody that doesn't exist can make me feel. My small hands turn to fists when I hear the word: Dad.

Mum carries what we need for the beach. She's so young but she remembers everything. Mum says it's because she's army trained. A neatly packed lunch. Sun oil. A folded grey army blanket with a stitched red hem. The army blanket had belonged to her dad, and it's great for the beach because it's worn so smooth the sand just falls away when you shake the blanket out at the end of the day. A book – from the library usually. New books cost too much. She reads whenever she can.

Luke and I carry rolled towels with our swimming shorts wrapped inside. Luke carries the plastic football (black and white hexagons).

We moved into the unfurnished, semi-detached house at the bottom of the cul-de-sac when I was four and Luke was seven. This was in 1968. Mum was in her mid-twenties, and had been on the housing list for four years, ever since she'd come back from London with Luke a month before I was born. There was no carpet on the stairs going from the front door up to the two bedrooms, but it was clean and newly painted. Did Mum paint the house before we moved in? There was a garden!

Before Mum got the house, we'd lived with her mum and dad in a small cottage right by the railway line. For those four years Mum and Nan shared a bed. I must have been in there with them at first. Then Luke and I shared the bed in the other room (I don't remember anything about living there, really, except for Stevie, the dark, short-haired tomboy in jeans who lived next door and who let me play with her sometimes). All that time, my Grandad Jim – a hard, kind, wooden-faced man with a large port-wine stain on his cheek who had been invalided out of the Royal Artillery a year after being rescued from the beach at Dunkirk – slept on a made-up bed on the kitchen floor.

I did not know, until nearly thirty years after he died, that Jim had never known his father – a stable hand who rented a room in the house Jim's mum lived in with her parents.

Jim joined the Royal Artillery as soon as he could. He may have lied about his age – the records, his discharge papers, are confusing – and gone in when he was just fifteen. Did he join the artillery because of the horses? The boy in his rough tunic, learning how to wash and soothe the horses. Transmissions of belonging and need passing between boy and horse.

Did the work feel like something remembered?

So gentle when I knew him, and Nan so sweet. Look, here are some animals. From her large black purse she gives Luke a polar bear, me a sea lion.

Towards the sea, everything is open light. Luke's eyes are wide with excitement. He's happiest when he's moving towards free space.

I can taste salt and hear gulls.

The warmth of the sun is too good. It's almost more than I can stand.

I am excited by everything I see, I can't help it: jet trails, the daylight moon. A jewel-like spider web suspended between the railings of an iron gate. At the centre of the web the dark spider is huge and terrifying, so big I think that I could disappear inside its moving black mouth.

I run to a house where the front garden is full of sunflowers.

It's the only house in the street with sunflowers. They have grown tall, and crowns of yellow flowers float high above my head. Sometimes I hear music coming from the house and one morning a girl and a boy – long-haired, barefoot, not much younger than Mum – were sitting outside reading and drinking wine.

A sunflower stretches the full length of itself in light. I stand hypnotized, feeling big and small at the same time. I say anything that comes into my head:

Ha, look at the sunflowers!

I really want Mum and Luke to look into the garden, and see what I see.

Mum's calling me. Her voice brings me back to an understanding of what is expected of me and how I should behave. My world re-forms and my place in it, my status as the youngest, the baby, becomes familiar once more.

I can't wait to get to the beach. At low tide, Luke will play football with me on the wet sand. There will be rock pools to look into, full of strawberry anemones and red-eyed velvet swimming crabs. Starfish and limpets. A different world beneath the breeze-riffled surface water. If the tide's in we'll swim straight away, and spend the morning bodysurfing on waves speeding to the shore.

I can't stop thinking about the sunflowers.

When I catch up to Mum she takes my hand, and we walk to the beach.

More than anything it's joy I want to put on her face and why I want her to look at the sunflowers.

Policemen live in specially allocated housing on Churchdale Road.

There are fewer police houses the closer you get to the beach, but I always feel like there's a policeman close by.

We leave the house and walk south together on Churchdale Road in the cool of early morning, the scent of honeysuckle and roses coming from the gardens, and leave the police houses behind. To get to the beach, we continue walking until we come to Seaside Road, by the Archery Tavern. Seaside Road is the way in and out of town. If you turn right here, and walk far enough, you come to the Regal Arcade and the Painted Wagon close to the town centre, where all the tough-behaving boys who live east of the Pier hang around on summer nights, smoking and spitting on the ground, waiting for something to happen. In a few years Luke will be one of the toughest boys in town. I'll only ever pretend to be tough.

I stand in front of flowers daydreaming, tell stories about things I haven't done. I do these things knowing they are wrong and hating myself for doing them, but unable to stop.

I want other boys to like me because that might give

the lie to what I know about myself. That I am worthless. That's why my dad left. If it wasn't for me, he wouldn't have left Mum and Luke and they'd still be happy. Dad knew about me before I was born. I wasn't worth sticking around for.

Near where we cross Seaside Road to get to Channel View Road is the hardware shop where one day I will steal a large, heavy knife with a big serrated blade and a black rubber handle that is sticky in my hand. Mum was paying for something she needed at the counter and the man wasn't thinking about me. Mum was good looking and the town, our part of it anyway, was the kind of place where everybody knew she was on her own.

I was so scared of being caught with the knife I stole – of a policeman leaving his house across the street from ours and, tucking in his white shirt as he walked, opening our gate and walking up the short path, maybe smelling Mum's roses while he waited for somebody to open the door, feeling sorry for Mum because she was young and pretty and kept nice roses and didn't deserve a son like me – that I threw the knife away before I could cut myself with it.

There are palm trees on Channel View Road. I love the soft whispering sound the high, green, feather-shaped leaves make when they move on the sea breeze. The breeze an ozonic perfume that always makes me joyous. As we get closer to the beach I begin to really taste the salt on the air, and hear the cries of countless gulls, wheeling now in snowy parabolas against the paling sky.

We always stay east of the Pier. We never go to the tourist beaches in town. Before the town existed, the beaches where we live were part of a fishing settlement called Sea Houses. There's still a small working fishing fleet, and I can hear the constant sweet chiming made by the rigging of the boats, and the sharp metallic scent of the fish stores.

I love the sound beach stones make under my feet. Sunlight on the limitless water suspends me, and the black hole I can feel growing inside, in a luminous gauze.

We look for a good place to put the blanket down. The beach at this early hour is almost deserted, but Mum's worried about boat tar and dog shit. Luke finds a clean place by the wooden groyne. We'll dive from the groyne later. Luke will go first so I know it's safe. The narrow beam beneath my feet will be slippery with green seaweed, the sun's heat sharp between my shoulder blades. Luke's back is dark in the same place, his wet head is sleek. I disappear into the space my brother makes in the water.

Part of me wants to have had the day already. I love going home in fading light, with the sun and salt on my skin so that I feel I am made from the beach. I need to get to that part of the day without anybody becoming unhappy. To be home having done nothing to be ashamed of and not having upset Mum.

This blanket is my sea house. Beyond it, the canted shingle beach, the cool clay-like sand at the shoreline, the foaming surf and water to the horizon, everything is free space that is permanently here and is mine to explore. I am a concentrate of sunlight, moving from rock pool to sand to water, the soft eternal waves fuzzing in my ears.

The sun's rise and fall changes the colour of the sky: the morning's fragile rose turns first to beaten gold and then to an almost transparently pale blue. More jet trails appear as rips in the sky before softly blossoming and then, slowly, disappearing.

We eat wrapped in towels. Shivering from the sea and warm at the same time, salt softening our skin, hair dripping with seawater. We don't talk much, just stare at the endless silver field of water, studded with slowly cresting, slowly falling points of light. Mum and Luke smile at me and I grin back (the sandy black and white football in my brother's lap).

Later, as late as possible, we will leave the beach under a sky becoming violet, the darkening sea at our backs.

Eastbourne, East Sussex, 1971

A big, suntanned man sleeps alone in Mum's bed. His hair fans out across her pillow. From a poster on Mum's wall Butch Cassidy and the Sundance Kid watch over the man as he sleeps. I hug the handle and the frame of the door and swing noiselessly into the room. The man in Mum's bed looks a lot like Sundance. Just like the Kid, the man's full sideburns and moustache are darker – red almost – than his fair hair. His sandy shoulders are splashed with freckles, like Luke's, like mine.

A summer morning, or the weekend. Either way I'm not at school. It's sunny. I run into Mum's room to see if we can go to the beach, but she's not there. When I see the man in the bed I want to curl up next to him.

Have I switched lives with another boy? Standing in honeyed light, Butch and Sundance smile down at me. They look the same as always, armed and dusty and cool, but there must be lots of people with that poster, even in this town. It's true Mum's is the most unfamiliar room in the house, the least known. I'm in all the other spaces, all the time, Luke too. Mum always tries to quiet us but our crashing progress through the house is uncontained. We fill the place up with our becoming, our undeniable boyhood. Mum's room is a made-space that's hers, and not to be tramped through by her sons. By its unfamiliarity I know it's hers.

But a man in Mum's bed, sleeping in the morning like it's the most natural thing in the world. There's never been a man in her bed before. Mum cared too much for us and worked too hard for love. I can hear her making breakfast in the kitchen, singing along to the soft pop music coming from her radio. It's great she's happy. I stare at the man. He has long eyelashes. He's big. I haven't been this close to a man before. He is breathing softly, and looks peaceful, like this is home. I am washed by the light where I stand. I can't speak. There's only one word I want to say and I can't say it

I don't know how to act around men. Once a year or so, Luke's godfather visits with his wife and son. Gough had been my dad's best friend but I don't think they see each other any more. Gough's married to a Spanish woman, Alejandra, and they live in Madrid. Their son, Mark, is my age. A pale, quiet boy haloed with long blonde hair, who sits close by his dad. Mark thinks he's better than us. I don't like him.

Gough's a dark, squat, powerful man. Bearded, black haired. He has a black belt in karate, and once he gave Luke a Polaroid of himself in a fighting stance on a flat terracotta roof – I guess his apartment – under a blue Mediterranean sky. I try hard to be noticed and liked but mostly Gough seems indifferent to me. I was jealous of Luke.

I don't know where my dad is. Jason – even the name's unfamiliar. I wonder if I have half-brothers and sisters somewhere. The mystery of shared blood and that there could be people living who look like you and are maybe even like you but you'll never know or meet them. Say he has another son – it's almost as if this other boy is me, in another world. Did my dad love him? And why was he with him and not me? Dad doesn't exist, but I fill my life with thinking about him.

I've heard nothing that will help me find him, which I'm constantly dreaming about. Mum's friend Viv, her blonde daughter Sally and their pug dog Dreamboat sometimes come around – the dog panting as he comes up the path. Viv floats up to our house. She's a welcome blast of noise and glamour. Viv's on her own, too, but she seems happy about it. Mum laughs more than usual when Viv visits, and sometimes has a drink and smokes a cigarette. They come to the beach with us sometimes. I like how Sally looks in her swimsuit. The blonde hair on her toffee-coloured arms. When Viv comes over Mum sometimes talks about Jason, and I sit quietly and try not to be noticed. The stories are all about his weakness. In his absence it's his insubstantiality that's talked about and reinforced for me. He lived on air and charm, Mum says.

I look into every man's face. Every man I meet could be him. I worry that we might walk past one another without realizing. If I miss him I might never get another chance.

My dreams are about finding him. About his restoration to me. The only thing better than finding him would be him coming for me. Lifting me up high onto his shoulders.

I hate my dad and love him and if he comes for me I will take his hand and go with him unquestioningly.

—

The man in the bed makes a soft sighing sound but does not move. Wake up, I think, wake up.

We'd been to see *Butch Cassidy and the Sundance Kid* for my birthday a couple of weeks before (or was it Luke's birthday?). I liked how Butch and Sundance were tough outlaws but everybody loved them, and how sunny it always seemed wherever they were. I wanted to live in their world and be like them. I thought my dad might be like Sundance.

When we played Butch and Sundance, Luke was always Butch because he got to choose, but I'd have been Sundance anyhow. The Kid was flash in the way he dressed – in Mum's poster he wears a dark suit and wide-brimmed dark hat, a leather waistcoat, an open-necked shirt. The dust on the suit tells you he's the real thing – he's not afraid to get dirty but he'll look good doing it. He makes his way through the world with a fast hand and a gun. The Kid's elegant stance is all challenge and dust and reality. Men just have to look at him and they put their guns away. The girl in the film looked like Mum.

Luke could make me cry by telling me that Butch gets away but Sundance dies at the end. I knew it wasn't true that either they both died or they both got away, but Luke could make me believe anything. It was around then that I started telling people I was American. Boys who punched me and called me names. Get up you bastard.

I'd spit blood into the dust and look up at the ugly ring of faces and tell them my dad was coming for me soon. My dad was somebody who would help me and show me what to do, so that the black hole inside would be filled with clear light. I'd live in America with him and we would ride horses.

For a few more seconds I stand looking at the man who looks like the Sundance Kid, and then I run downstairs to find Mum and Luke.

The Sundance Kid drove us on the coast road west to the Cuckmere River valley. We travelled in a wash of southern light that filled the car and seemed to push at and past the edges of the world. The unfolding road flat then rising then falling through glossy green downland. To the south the sea shone like stamped tin.

We would have looked good in that car. A young handsome suntanned family. The big young man confident behind the wheel. The pretty dark-haired woman next to him. Two cute boys in the back. If there had been a dog, a blond Lab, sticking his head out the window, we would have looked perfect. People would have said: I want to be part of that family. I liked the idea of people watching us drive past but on that road there was nobody to see.

Luke was cool. He kept his distance. Because of this coolness the man talked to Luke like an equal. Men always did.

Any car would have seemed fast. If I'd been in a car before I don't remember it – but I'm sure the red car was a sports car, and that the Sundance Kid drove fast, and carried on driving fast and laughing with Mum until I asked him to stop so that I could be sick.

I was sick before he stopped. I got sick the way a young dog gets sick or wets itself from excitement. I couldn't wait for the man to stop the car. When he did, near the beach,

Mum got me out of my clothes and wrapped me in her dad's old grey blanket. Luke and the Kid walked across the road to the beach and threw stones into the sea.

Eastbourne, East Sussex, 1975

Ready? Luke says.

This high up, I can see as far as Beachy Head. The chalk cliffs are distant, peachy slabs in the afternoon light. I'm above the tourist beaches, the seafront gardens full of blooms and the white hotels. Summer crowds fill the beaches and the terraced promenade. A seagull, shockingly large, coasts past and seems to look at me. More gulls ride the thermals. The railing is cold against my back. I press my bare heels so hard to the Pier's edge I can feel the indentations the stubbly concrete makes on my skin. My toes stick over the edge. I lean back against the rail. There's nothing but sun-warmed, empty space in front of me.

It's high tide, and all along the length of the Pier there are kids – boys mostly but some girls – diving and jumping into the sea. Local kids – you can tell us by how dark we are. There's Gary Angelino – without his skateboard – monkey-faced, headful of blond curls, jumping with a yell and disappearing into the water.

The sky is thick with falling kids and white birds.

Far below me the sea sucks at the pylons. Luke reckons it's at least a sixty-foot drop. There are goosebumps on my arms and chest but I can't see any on Luke's smooth, sun-darkened skin.

More gulls float past. Warm air or not, I'm shivering.

What's beyond the curved horizon?

Luke looks at me. Splash of freckles across his dark face. He's thirteen – he'll be fourteen later this month. I'm just eleven. It's at this time of year – just after my birthday in May and before Luke's in July – that I feel closest to him. I'm already as tall as he is and I know that soon I'll be taller, but I always think he's bigger than me.

You've done it before. Right?

We are barefoot, wearing cut off-jeans, hair to our shoulders.

Loads of times. That's what you told Gaz.

I can't remember what my brother's voice sounded like before it broke.

I have.

Come on then.

Luke is the son Jason left. He hadn't left me, I didn't exist. Secretly I always worry that one day my brother will blame me for Dad leaving. Luke doesn't talk about how he feels (and he's got an overbite that makes him look like he's holding on to what he's really thinking). The more important something is to him the less likely he is to talk about it. We never talk about Dad. Maybe we don't need to. Luke's the only one who knows what I feel. He never complains about having to look after me when Mum's at work. At home later, he'll let me lie down with my head in his lap while we watch TV.

Mostly though, I just want to be like him. I want to do what he does.

—

The kids already in the sea are looking up at those of us at the rail and shouting and making wanker signs. My heart's thumping so loudly I can't hear what they're saying. Either side of us at the rail more kids jump, dark falling shapes against the pale sky. They smash into the water far below. Each entry point becomes a crown of rising water. A boy called Donny lands on his back and screams and the other kids laugh at him. Steve, a big-eared kid I go to school and play football with, throws a huge black inner tube over the side and then jumps after it. If I don't jump everybody will know. Luke will understand but he'll be ashamed.

Luke smiles at me. He is full of joy – for his life, for this moment, this shared and taught action. His smile transforms his face that is most often watchful. The face of a boy with secret plans he's not going to tell you about.

Don't think about it, he says, just jump. Keep your feet together so your balls don't hit the water.

This is before the police start coming to the house at night looking for him. When he hadn't come home and his bed was empty I was scared he'd been taken away. Who'd look after me then?

I'd listen for the gate. If I fell asleep without hearing it open, I knew I'd wake up to find Luke in bed. We could both open the gate without making a sound. If I heard the gate late at night, if the sound of it opening woke me, I'd know it was the police.

The second time I was arrested – Luke had left for India by then – a policeman wearing a thick uniform that smelled of sweat said: Aren't you Luke's brother? When I said yes he looked pleased with himself. The cell was painted the same grey colour as the thin blanket on the cot. A thousand boys had carved their names into the walls. I looked for Luke's name, but it wasn't there.

I remember Luke's eyes shining when he came back from India for the first time. Did he tell me about the Himalayan Valley of Flowers (unending meadows full of poppies and orchids, wild bees and clouds of butterflies)?

I jump a split second after Luke.

With his bright grin, sun-lightened hair and honeyed skin he is light falling in light.

I'm falling too, but it's okay because Luke is with me.

Eastbourne, East Sussex, 1977

Pete was tattooed at fourteen. While the rest of us were cutting ourselves, or making handmade tattoos with India ink, Pete had been to a proper shop up in Croydon, where his nan lived.

A tattooist called Ian Frost put on a classic eagle and a black panther, one on each forearm, big and in full colour. 'Frostie' Frost was well known for his black panthers and eagles. The outlines were solid and the colours were bright. The eagle swooped with talons bared. The panther was a mass of dark muscle and power. Frostie had tattooed red lines coming from the panther's claws, like the big cat was cutting into Pete's arm.

Tattoos were considered dirty and criminal. Sailors, bikers, Borstal boys got tattooed. Troublemakers of all kinds. What I loved most about tattoos was the toughness they seemed to give to the boys who had them. I hung out at the Regal Arcade and studied the tough boys. I pierced my ear. Cut crucifixes into my arms. I smoked.

I'm forgetting how familiar tattoos were. Grandad had an Artillery tattoo, blue and faded. Hilary, the big, gentle biker who lived next door to us with his mum and dad, was heavily tattooed with daggers and death-heads.

I can't see Pete's tattoos where he's standing. It's dusk, and he's outside the Rose and Crown with the fiery light of just before dark behind him, so that his hulking figure is a fuzzed, dark mass. In any light he looks much older than the kid he is. I'm facing the pub with an unlit cigarette in my mouth. The pub is what I see.

Already the starlings have disappeared from the sky. Soon the dusk will turn to darkness, and it will be Friday night.

Like me, Pete has an older brother. I don't know if it's this that makes us want to be out where our brothers are on Friday nights. I imagine the night is like the beach, a free space where you can do and be what you want.

Friday nights are for drinking, fighting and picking up girls. We've heard the stories, now we need to find out.

The unlit cigarette feels fat in my mouth. A boy called Spike gave me my first cigarette when I was eleven. Spike was an acne-scarred, crop-headed boy who came drunk to class and got into fights and was finally expelled when he was sixteen. He always had loads of cigarettes that he passed around to boys who would take them. Spike killed himself when he was eighteen. The story was that his dad had been raping him for years. I guess it was his dad who gave him the cigarettes. Maybe Spike was supposed to bring other boys to the place where he lived with his dad.

Spike showed me the three Ks hidden on the packet design that proved the Ku Klux Klan owned Marlboro. Spike also showed me how to carefully pull away and burn a hole in the cellophane from the bottom of the pack, and then blow smoke into the hole. When Spike gently tapped the cellophane and little smoke rings came out I thought it was cool.

When you're a kid, you don't think boys like Spike are

the way they are because of what an adult has done to them. You just think that's how they are.

I take the cigarette out of my mouth, put it back, and light up. I lean over and light Pete up too. This close I can see his cool grey eyes.

You ready? Pete says.

I was wearing a tight Three Star tank top with a rouched waist, under a Falmer jean jacket. Dark blue three-button high-waist baggies with a huge flare – the trousers really tight on my arse. My shoulder-length red hair was cut in a feather cut.

After my bath I'd towel-dried my hair and then used Mum's blow dryer to get the right windblown look. I'd brought Mum's full-length mirror into my and Luke's room and I stood in front of it for a long time. I told Mum I was seeing some friends but I know she thought I was going to meet a girl.

Pete was dressed pretty much the same as me. He carried his jean jacket so his tattoos could be seen. I thought we looked like two young workers – apprentices maybe – dressed up and out for a good time on a Friday night.

The most important part of the outfit was Luke's platform shoes. I was already five foot ten and the shoes added another three inches to my height.

I don't remember what I had to give or promise Luke to get him to lend me the shoes. Maybe nothing because he didn't wear them any more. The month before, in April 1977, the Clash had released their first album. Luke was wearing his hair chopped and spiked. Combat trousers, ripped T-shirts and DMs. I was too preoccupied to realize the world had changed, that nothing would ever be the same.

The pub door is partly open. Past the threshold, dark geometric shapes are made by the floorboards and the panelled wood bar. On the floor is a large Cinzano ashtray full of water. The water is moon-radiant against the round white plastic inlay of the ashtray and the dark expanse of the floor.

Different coloured spirits seem to pulse in their bottles. At the limit of my vision half a man is sitting on half a red stool. He's wearing half a check jacket. There's a feather in the band of the worn green hat he's placed on the bar.

Throwing our cigarettes on the ground and blowing out smoke, we walk slowly through the open doorway of the pub. The light is all behind us now. The pub is cool and quiet.

The man in the check jacket is the only drinker in there. Pete picked the Rose and Crown because it wasn't near the seafront and it wasn't in town. It's on a quiet street called Langney Road. The man at the bar is drinking an amber spirit in a round glass and reading the racing results in the *Evening Argus*. Absently his fingers play with the worn feather in his hat. He doesn't look up. Drinking alone in every town are men whose youth and fire once made them princes.

The barman was an old Ted. Quiff grey but still thick. Slicked back. Squared-off sideburns. Pale-blue eyes. A white shirt with the sleeves folded to his pale elbows. Blue faded tattoos. Brewery tie and tie-clip. He put his cigarette in the ashtray. A chunky ID bracelet on his right wrist clicked against the bar.

Yes lads, he said.

Light and bitter please, I said.

Light and bitter – three-quarters of a pint of Harvey's Sussex Best Bitter with a bottle of light, or pale ale – was my grandad's drink. I thought it made me sound older – like I knew what I was talking about.

The same, Pete said.

We took our drinks over to the table by the door.

Pete took out his cigarettes and gave me one. I lit us both. I poured light ale into my glass, tilting the glass so that the beer wouldn't foam up. I remember the moving ruby light that was the beer in my glass.

I took a drink of beer, then another.

The anger I carried was always there so I never expected to feel any different.

Anger was a monster living inside me, feeding on absence.

My dad didn't want me because I'm shit.

Drinking made the monster go away. The first taste. I couldn't believe it. This will protect me from what I feel.

I looked at my glass, admiring the shining beer in it, then picked it up and took another drink. Another flare into the darkness. This was great.

This is fucking great, I said.

Keep it cool, Pete said.

What was wrong with him. Didn't he get it?

I started laughing.

What's the matter with you? Pete said.

Nothing, I said, still laughing. I was so taken with how tough Pete's tattoos looked, I hadn't noticed how beautiful they were.

I was relaxed. A weight had been taken from me. Something new had begun.

Eastbourne, East Sussex, 1979

Ponyboy Curtis walks from the darkness of the movie house into a sunlit American afternoon. Old navy sweatshirt with cut-off sleeves, jeans and sneakers. Long red hair greased back. Thinking about Paul Newman and a ride home, Ponyboy walks off the edge of the page, taking a piece of my teenage heart with him.

Tierney is sleeping. Her lamb-white hair is still dark with sweat at the roots. What's she dreaming of? The room is hot and smells of us. Luke's bed is empty. I read the end of *The Outsiders* again. Ponyboy struggling how to write his story when he's never seen stories about boys like him – greasers, *white trash* – written down any place.

Hey Ponyboy, wait up!

Tierney yawns and stretches beside me. Her T-shirt rides up, showing her white stomach and knickers and soft pad of hair underneath. She opens her grey eyes.

I really have to go home, she says in her low voice.
I thought you were asleep.

I have to go home, Ponyboy says, Darry will kill me if I'm late again.

I was, Tierney says, why didn't you wake me?

Your brother doesn't hate you Pony, he just worries about you. I wish we could talk some more – there's something I need to tell you.

Ow! Fuck, Tierney!

Why didn't you wake me?

I don't know.

On the beach, it's the fragments of girls that kill you. Bikini-strap lines. Sweat and oil pooled in an arched back. Sand and broken shells sticking to hot bodies. There's so much tight brown skin so close to my hands and mouth it hurts. The girls burn into my mind.

Tierney's skin is milk-coloured, even in the summer. It's her fairness that drives me crazy. Tierney's not a beach girl, except at night when we've got nowhere else to be together. I burn, she says, pinching skin on her thigh so that it goes red. Like *that*.

Tierney's a loner like me. A dreaming, often sad, long-legged girl in a pale T-shirt and a short, weightless rah-rah skirt – the skirt on the floor by the bed, with the bag she carries her sketchbooks and pens in. Her hair is long, and she's self-conscious about how fine it is. Sometimes she crimps it to make it look thicker. Tonight her hair is a burst of white zigzags. There's a sweet bump on the bridge of her nose that makes it look broken. Her pale lips are sometimes dry.

She takes care of me when I get drunk and go crazy because there's something urgent I need to understand but I don't know what it is. I don't know what I give her.

Why are you angry at your mum?

I'm not.

Yeah, you are. It makes *me* angry.

I knew what Tierney said was true but until she said it I didn't know I was or why. In my heart I loved Mum all the time.

I tell Tierney about the black hole and the monster who lives inside it.

You're lucky, she says. I wish my dad wasn't there.

Tierney grabs the book from me and starts flicking through it.

What's it about?

Tierney pushes me away.

Stop kissing me and tell me, she says.

I keep kissing her all over. I push my face against her knickers. Blow a hot breath against the pad of hair.

She hits me, laughing. I kiss her mouth. She tastes of strawberry lip balm and me.

Tell me!

OK, OK, I say. Ponyboy's our age, with long red hair slicked back and grey-green eyes. He's from the wrong side of the tracks. He lives with his brothers Darry and Sodapop. Darry's the oldest and he's in charge. They're all greasers.

What happened to Ponyboy's parents?

They died in a car wreck. The brothers are always scared the family will be split up and Ponyboy will be put in a home.

Ponyboy thinks his brother Darry doesn't love him. He'd rather be like his friend Johnny Cade, whose parents don't care about him at all. When Darry hits him for staying out late, Ponyboy decides to run away. It's late but he finds Johnny sleeping in the park.

Ponyboy and Johnny get jumped by a carload of drunk Socs – the rich kids in the town. They hold Pony's head under the water in the fountain. Johnny's so scared Pony's going to die, he stabs and kills one of the rich kids.

Poor Johnny, Tierney says. Then what happens?

I tell her.

When he sits down to write his story, Ponyboy begins like this: 'When I stepped out into the bright sunlight from the darkness of the movie house, I had only two things on my mind: Paul Newman and a ride home . . .'

You talk about him like you love him, Tierney says.

What I wanted to tell you was I didn't know there were other boys like me. I thought I was on my own for ever.

You're not alone, Ponyboy says. Remember what I said, about the hundreds and hundreds of boys on the wrong side of the tracks, who watch sunsets and look at stars and dream of something better?

I learnt that from reading Johnny's letter – the one I found after he died. You remember what he said: Don't be so bugged over being a greaser. You still have a lot of time to make yourself be what you want. It was reading his letter that made me want to tell my story in the first place. Written lives are visible and have power.

Tierney's looking at the book as I dream.

A girl wrote this book! she says. A seventeen-year old girl!

I know, I say.

I try and make out it doesn't matter, but when I found out a girl had made Ponyboy and all the other boys in the book I was struck by lightning.

A girl had imagined Ponyboy – his thoughts were her thoughts. She had made the boys and their world so real it was burned into my mind for ever. Like the girls on the beach. Like Tierney. Somehow because a girl – a teenage girl – had written the book made the feeling that I wanted to write my own stories even stronger.

What do you think about that? Tierney says. A girl. I bet you thought it was somebody tough.

I need to get you out of here, I say. Luke will be home soon.

I do up my jeans and pull on my sweatshirt. I push back my red hair.

Tierney laughs. She reaches for her skirt, and pulls it over her legs. She ties back her frizzy hair with a scrunchie.

You're crazy Ponyboy, she says.

Eastbourne, East Sussex, 1982

Johann, wearing a black leather jacket with *Muerte a Los Comunistas* painted over where his heart is, drinks some beer and says he's almost finished working on a series of sun paintings. Straight black hair frames a dark face that's all hard-looking planes and edges. Hawk nose and shining eyes. Johann's older than us – twenty-odd to our seventeens and eighteens – and already married, to Kit, and they have a baby son and another kid on the way. They live out at Alfriston – in the countryside – and Johann works as a gardener. Kit's a painter too.

All summer, Johann says. Before work and after work. There's bloody loads of them, he laughs. In the baby's room, everywhere. The suns all come out different.

Driftwood, paper, wood board, canvas sometimes but canvas is expensive, he says. I found a big piece of sailcloth when I was working in Fairlight. Kit washed it to get the salt out and stuck it on the line with the nappies – I'm going to try some acrylics on it.

Johann says: What about you? What are you doing?

I don't know Johann well and he doesn't know me. He knows Steve, because Steve's going out with Kit's little sister, Oona, and he knows, or I think he knows, that I'm Steve's friend. I don't know him well enough to ask why he's wearing that jacket, and besides, Johann has a reputation for being a tough nut.

I say that often I do not feel present, but Johann doesn't hear me in the Friday night noise of the bar. He turns his head to say something to Ashley, and I am amazed to see that the black rope of his hair reaches almost to his waist.

Summer's over. Soon I'll be leaving Eastbourne. Leaving these friends. Leaving Steve.

I'm going to London. The others have talked about it but I'm going.

I've been trying to write the sun on the sea but I can't get it right. The words moving in endless helices behind my eyes often seem more real, more present, than what's in front of me, so that not getting the words right feels dangerously like not getting my life right.

Do you know what I mean? I say to Johann.

Johann says, I like the doing of it, mostly. Each time is different. I think it pays not to be too uptight. I don't expect to get anything right.

Which sounds like the things Steve says, then I think maybe he heard them from Johann first. There always has to be a source.

If I feel like painting, Johann says, I'm gonna paint.

Ashley's Levi's have a huge, deliberate-looking hole in the crotch, showing off the swell of his balls under snow-white pants, and a splash of tanned thigh. Ashley's just started a band. He's going to write the songs and play guitar. We're all crowded round the big wooden table by the lighted window that looks out onto the street and Ashley, his shining pop-star hair that he has trained to fall into his eyes falling into his eyes, sits on show in the gilded frame.

I've been trying to write the slowly rising, slowly falling terraces of water studded with infinite points of light. And two boys there, playing on the beach at low tide, twin dark forms rimmed by the same illumination.

Am I wrong to think there's some definite way to write the light on the water – or the fire-coloured light in this bar, shining in the black corrugations of Johann's leather jacket and the glasses of beer on the table?

The table is littered with torn-up and sketched and scribbled-on beer mats, empty cigarette packets, a yellow Pernod ashtray heaped with butts, some red with lipstick, Steve's copy of Jack Kerouac's *Mexico City Blues* that I have failed to understand, and that I should have kept in a bag so that I wouldn't have to keep moving it away from spilled beer, only I want people to see me with it – even though the boys that matter will know the book isn't mine. I drink some beer and laugh, thinking that I should tell Steve that the table looks like the inside of my head, only Steve isn't here yet.

Everybody's talking about Jack Kerouac but I'm still reading Hemingway. I'm hung up on his hard surfaces that do not yield to me. Dark chaos swirls beneath the words Hemingway allows himself to use. I'm infatuated by what he doesn't say. By what I bring to his white spaces.

My life in its moment by moment progression feels so uncertain – so unknowable in its absences, so that I feel, mostly, that I am free-falling – that I can't lose control even when I'm drunk. I'm locked in. I know this is a weakness. I need to let go. Find meaning in the chaos. I'm pretty sure that's what Johann means, and why Steve gave me *Mexico*

City Blues to read. 242 poems like this one – just opening the book at random because nobody's talking to me:

> *The wheel of the quivering meat*
> > *conception*
> *Turns in the void expelling human beings,*
> *Pigs, turtles, frogs, insects, nits,*
> *Mice, lice, lizards, rats, roan*
> *Racinghorses*

And so on.

> *All the endless conception of living*
> > *beings*
> *Gnashing everywhere in Consciousness*
> > (211th Chorus)

> *The sound in your mind*
> *is the first sound*
> *that you could sing*
> (242nd Chorus).

I'm not brave enough to say what's in my mind, and I think I drink all this beer so I don't have to face what I really feel. It's why I didn't take acid this summer, when Steve and all the others did, because I knew I'd have to face feeling if I did, and I was frightened. I might be imagining this, but I think not taking acid is the reason Johann and the others don't take me seriously.

Steve's the only one who understands. 'I've taken it with Johann and Ashley, a couple of weeks ago,' he wrote to me. We write each other letters all the time. My letters are urgent and confessional, Steve's seem to be full of the first thing that comes into his head: incantatory rhymes and stories that confuse and frustrate me. I just want him to say he loves me.

'I shall describe everything to you another time,' he wrote. 'They've taken it a couple of times since. I won't. Maybe sometime, not at the moment. Everything is brilliant anyway. Just brilliant. I'm in love' (he means with Oona).

> *all the black*
> *tunnels of hate*
> *or love I'm falling*
> *through, are*
> *really radiant*
> *right eternities*
> *for me*
> (184th Chorus)

I've only got a couple of cigarettes left and I'm saving one for Steve because he never has any. If he doesn't come soon, I'm going to have to smoke the one I'm saving for him.

I'm always early and Steve's always late. I know my constant need to know what things mean sometimes wears him out. Sometimes he's not home when I call – especially now he's with Oona.

I try not to go round to Steve's every day, and I'm always scared he won't be in when I do call. His big-eared outline coming near, darkening and filling the glass pane of his front door, floods me with love and relief.

I'm a bit scared by the art-student girls like Oona who float around Steve and Ashley. They all look the same – hair cut severely short, bright-red lipstick, small breasts. They wear tight gingham dresses, or pedal-pushers, or short denim skirts over black wool tights, DM shoes or Kung-Fu slippers, cute suede moccasins.

The girls seem tuned in only to Steve and Ashley – the boys at the centre. The cool looks I get from these girls tell me I'm an outlier. They look right into me and know what I want.

I work my way through the crowd of more art students to the bar. We're not art students. Apart from Johann, we're all on the dole. I'm wearing a striped fisherman shirt, hand-washed and sun-dried to soften it, like Hemingway said. Levi's and espadrilles. My summer tan is only now starting to fade, so my skin is still dark, but cool. My red hair is sun-streaked almost to gold.

See the jacket he's wearing?

There are three of them, all wearing black shirts buttoned to the neck, black trousers and black DM shoes. One of them's wearing black nail polish. Asymmetrical haircuts – dyed black and shaved close on one side and long on the other.

It's really too much, the boy with black nail polish says. Somebody should say something. I mean it's really an outrage.

Tierney's working behind the bar, her hair phosphorescent under the light. She's wearing a white peasant blouse and cut-off jeans. She pours me a beer, doesn't charge me.

You look like a pirate, she says, and then mouths at me: Don't get drunk.

When I drink I don't know which boy will appear. The angry boy who fights and cries, or the boy who talks and talks about the latest book or record Steve's given him or the books and records he's increasingly discovering for himself. The first boy had scared Tierney away. The second boy sometimes wins her back for a short time.

He's here! Suddenly standing next to me at the crowded bar, wearing a dazzling cotton shirt and I think of a sail, of Johann's sailcloth, and the sun he wants to paint on it. I'm a clean boy but I've never known a boy as clean as Steve. He's light to my dark.

Where've you been? I've been waiting for you, I let out, which is the wrong thing to say and Steve doesn't answer. Big ears and Greek curls. Thick powerful neck. His smiling grey eyes light up his square, strong-jawed face.

It's impossible to think I can have Steve for myself but at least tonight he hasn't got Oona with him, who quite rightly hates me or at least is jealous because of the amount of time Steve spends with me, which isn't that much.

I knew him when we were little kids. We were both really good at football, although in proper matches Steve had more confidence than me and was the better player.

Then I lost track of him – he's a year older – and when I found him again, when I was fifteen or so and he was sixteen, he seemed fully formed.

Steve's a prince in his house – he's an only child: clean handkerchief every day and drawers full of white socks, and with a room next to the kitchen (a whole room to himself, separate from his bedroom, which is really just an austere cell, it's true) where he keeps his LPs and record player and a glass-fronted bookcase full of books. There's even a serving hatch to the kitchen and every so often it whooshes open and his mum pushes through cups of tea and cheese sandwiches, made with tomatoes she grows in her garden and ripens on the kitchen windowsill. I am always so hungry for what Steve gives me that it becomes mixed in with a more general hunger and I wolf down the tea and sandwiches, while outside, the day goes on. Tomatoes turn from green to red on the sill, flowers open, tides change.

Now this, Steve says — holding the black disc of Big Youth's *Screaming Target* slanted between his palms, flipping it over, never touching the surface of the record, his movements practised, delicate, putting it on the turntable, lifting the stylus and decisively blowing fluff from the needle, putting the needle on the record with the softest of crunches – is fucking brilliant.

Sonic fuzz. Silence, voice, a story, a scream that makes me jump, rat-rat-rat, a brilliant hesitation, melody. I've heard this song before but not this *version*:

No, no no, begins the singer, but Big Youth interrupts, he wants yes, not no:

What you say no well I say yeah, cos you should never say no

I feel my sense of self, who I am and always will be, float up and disperse out into Steve's room and fold into basslines thick as my heartbeat, ghost voices, fragments of melody, Big Youth's words that I understand hardly at all but it doesn't matter, I'm free-floating. The self that returns to me has been changed for ever by three minutes of music. Doors open that can never be closed. The kettle whistles.

Steve's mum pushes cups of tea through the serving hatch.

Ooh Steve, she says, that's enough to drive anybody mad.

Steve laughs. This is even better, he says, taking Donny Hathaway's *Extension of a Man* from its sleeve.

None of us have dads – not Johann or Steve or Ashley or me. None of us have dads and all of us are looking for something. Was there a connection? There had to be. It was Steve who gave me *On the Road*, and what are Sal and Dean searching for after all if not for their fathers – absent in death and life? If you didn't have a dad who loved you, or who beat you when he came home drunk, I'm not stupid, then you were always looking for him, or something else.

Steve didn't seem marked by not having a dad in the way I felt myself to be, like a shark had torn away a great chunk of me. Maybe he was able to hide abandonment, and maybe he didn't feel abandoned. I didn't know who I was. Steve said that meant I could be anybody I wanted. Steve seemed to enjoy as freedom the absence that haunted me. Good looks and a big cock gave him confidence to be in the world – maybe it was as simple as that.

All right? he says, and laughs his great laugh, explosive and generous. He looks at me now, like I'm the source of his joy, and underneath the laugh and in his look I recognize affection, but also Steve's awareness of my need, about which he can be more or less tolerant depending on his mood. I've placed him so high, I think he feels a great responsibility not to let me down – and sometimes he is sullen about this, and breaks my heart.

Steve gets it that my need is about wanting to know what he knows, but of course he can't tell me what he knows, any more than he'll ever be able to describe his acid trip – I'm going to have to do that for myself if I ever want to know – and so his laugh has exasperation at my stupidity folded into it. I'm happy that tonight his hello is affectionate and even loving, I guess because he's not with Oona and so doesn't have to take care of both of us, with all the weary division of attention that involves, but also because I'm so open about how great I think he is (Oona isn't, at least not publicly, she guards him coolly). Who doesn't want to be adored?

But yes, I know that Steve always partly wants me to leave him alone so he can be with boys like Johann and Ashley who don't need things explaining to them.

'There's a lot of aboutness going on,' he wrote to me. 'Desire deflected to speeches *about* desire.'

Got a cigarette?

I give Steve a cigarette and take one for me, my last. He gets a beer from Tierney. She smiles at him and I'm not jealous.

Can I have a couple of cigarettes, Tierney?

I've got to have cigarettes if, like I hope to, I end up walking home with Steve, because at some point we'll stop, and look at the sea and talk, and then we'll both want to smoke.

After I've taken a cigarette for me and Steve, Tierney's only got four left. Do I beg off Tierney too much?

I always get drunk more quickly than everybody else. I'd be early to wherever the boys were meeting up, and often I didn't know, unless Steve told me, but really there were only one or two bars in town we went to – all the other pubs, like the Painted Wagon and the Hunting Lodge, are full of men who call us freaks and queers, and who would attack Ashley on sight for the way he's dressed tonight – but sometimes Steve and the others meet up elsewhere, to take acid, for example, and if I hear about it later I get angry and wonder if I've been left out deliberately. I'm impatient to be in the night and in the company of my friends, and in a rush to meet this new person I am becoming, but I always get drunk too quickly, and during the best part, the centre of the evening, I am there and not there.

We move back through the crowd to the table by the window.

How beautiful these boys are, my friends.

Am I beautiful? I think I must be. Even if I am drunk.

There's a big crush now.

Everybody's talking at once.

Everybody's happy to see Steve. His white shirt is so bright.

I point at the mess on the table, say to Steve, It looks like the inside of my head. Steve smiles.

The boys in black shirts keep giving us dirty looks.

There's going to be trouble over Johann's jacket, I say. Why's he wearing it?

Steve laughs and says – I don't know!

But I know he does. Johann and Ashley and Steve keep looking at each other and laughing.

The three boys in black shirts are suddenly at our table. Two of them hang back but the leader, the boy with black painted fingernails and, I can see now, an acne-scarred face, is furious.

If that's a joke it's in pretty poor taste.

Everybody starts shouting at once.

The boy with painted fingernails shouts something about death squads in El Salvador and Ireland and Bobby Sands. Slogans follow slogans. Thatcher and the mass unemployed.

Yes, Ashley shouts, but is Carraway queer for Gatsby?

Black Nail Polish lunges for Johann, and in a flash there's a red water pistol in Johann's hands. Steve and Ashley draw their own guns and fire at the boys in black shirts and then at everybody else. There's water everywhere. The art students' asymmetrical haircuts are ruined. We all get kicked out.

On the seafront, I want another drink. I've got just enough money for me and Steve. The only place open is the bar of the Burlington Hotel, which is a gay bar.

Come on Steve, I say, and we walk through a revolving door into the quiet, almost empty dark room. There are a few men sitting in high-backed chairs and I can only see the tops of their heads. Even so I sense that these men have made themselves still as Steve and I come in, too loudly.

Gorgeous George is behind the bar. All the kids know him. He's been around for ever. I remember coming off the beach one sun-blasted afternoon, and going into the pub near the seafront, the Cavalier, where Gorgeous George was then working. I was with a girl called Fawn, who wore a string bikini top and a beach towel around her waist. Her blonde hair was wet and tied up. I was wearing cut-offs and nothing else. I was dark and my hair was to my shoulders.

Ooh, said Gorgeous George.

His platinum-coloured hair and gold-framed glasses shine in the darkness.

Get out, he says, before I've even said anything.

We don't want your sort in here causing trouble.

Steve starts laughing but I want a drink.

Give us a drink, you old poof, I shout.

Gorgeous George comes out from behind the bar and starts pushing me and Steve towards the door. I let myself be pushed. We all go through the revolving door and out onto the deserted street. The sea on the other side of the road is an infinitely pleated field of dark movement.

I turn and hit George and he falls into the revolving doors and the doors move round and slowly carry him back inside the bar.

Steve and I run laughing along the front towards home.

We are standing by Seaside Rec, where tonight we will separate. Sometimes I go out of my way and walk all the way to Steve's house. The rec is a dark flat expanse, you can barely see the block of toilets that, a couple of years before, when I was still a kid, I tagged with big red graffiti saying ARSENAL RULE and NORTH BANK.

Your sort, Steve says.

Fuck, I say.

Come here, Steve says.

When Steve holds me, I feel a shift inside. I have to consider that my fear that I'm worthless and the desperation to prove I'm not have given me an intensity that is attractive to him – and maybe to the other boys – in the same way their coolness is something I want for myself.

When we kiss, Steve is a girl (is he kissing a girl, too?), and at the same time a boy. I have a split-second vision of the two of us naked, of me stroking his cock. Then I disappear so that the world is our kiss. There is nothing else. Then I see sunflowers. Then I open my eyes and look into Steve's grey eyes.

I go to kiss him again, or he moves to kiss me, and one of us moves his head, so that instead of kissing, Steve's head smacks into my eye.

Shit! Shit!

In the morning the eye is swollen and closed tight. Mum doesn't believe I haven't been fighting.

Unknown

Jason's tailored single-breasted suit jacket fits him beautifully. The jacket is buttoned – a modern three buttons rather than the more traditional two. The material has a sheen, which might be something to do with where Jason's standing and the distribution of light in the room (the part of the lacquered or just thickly painted wall panel he's standing in front of shines, too, although not elsewhere) but might also mean that the suit is made from some kind of silk and mohair blend (a *tonic* suit). Thin lapels, lush carnation. Tight, dark tie. Breast-pocket handkerchief a snowy peak. His shirt collar is radiant, and round at the tips.

My dad dressed to the nines in the only picture I have of him. Mum sent it to me out of the blue. Jason's already living in the 60s – the decade that's just begun when this picture was taken. Look at that round collar! Half an inch of sparkling shirt-cuff shows below the jacket's left sleeve. He wears a thick wedding ring – is it a wedding ring? It looks too large but it's on the third finger of his left hand so it must be? His fingers look oddly swollen and soft.

Mum said: I always knew he was up to no good. His friends were dodgy. Nobody had a real job. The girlfriends were all gorgeous. Balenciaga models, Roedean girls. We'd go to the 21 Club – a gambling place in Mayfair – the gangster Billy Hill had a stake in it.

The photo is black and white and thick as a postcard, otherwise it might not have lasted this long, and there are half-moon indentations in each corner that tell me it was taken out of a photo album. White borders like a postcard, too. The number 4208 is printed – slanted left to right – on the back, followed by a pencil written slash and the number 6.

Gough and Alejandra on their wedding day. Jason is best man. Jason's shorter than Gough and shorter than Alejandra too, though she is probably wearing heels, but that's the first thing I noticed. How small and young he seems. Really, if it wasn't for the way he's dressed he'd look about seventeen.

Gough's right hand is in his pocket, his left is just visible at Alejandra's waist. Unlike Jason his suit jacket is open. You can see that his tie – what looks like thick uneven bands of different colours – is squared off at the end. He is looking down, not at Alejandra exactly, but as though he's listening. Because he's smiling, he's the only one in the picture who looks fully present. He has a moustache-less beard – his cheeks are clean shaved and look flushed. Compared to Jason he looks old-fashioned but solid. More grown up. Jason has a weak chin, too, though that could just be how the camera has caught him.

Alejandra, her veil drawn back (she's wearing a veil! – actually the strangest detail in the picture, it seems pinned to the top of her head by a corsage, the flowers almost as large as her face), hair down to her shoulders, is expressionless. She does not look happy. Maybe she is tired of having her picture taken, though in the next second she could be smiling. She is looking, not at the camera but at something or somebody beyond the photographer. Her arms are bare – her hands clasped in front of the patterned lace skirt of her dress so that you can't see her wedding ring – though that might be it, that tiny something that might be a mark on her dress, below the outsized knuckles of her left hand. She wears two bracelets on her right arm – one on her wrist and one higher up on her forearm.

It's true that Alejandra's expression is close to vacant, and her mouth is set, but you can see how pretty she is.

Maybe she doesn't like Jason!

Who took the picture? Mum?

Jason's holding a note in his right hand, which also holds a too-big cigar dangerously close to Alejandra's skirt. Jason's touching or feeling the note between the thumb and forefinger of his left hand. More precisely, the money or piece of paper is held between the thumb and forefinger of both hands. The cigar in the right hand makes it look as though that's the hand that also holds the paper.

Is it a telegram of congratulation from someone who couldn't make the wedding? There are some torn-open envelopes on the table. Does the paper contain his notes for a speech? Is he making the speech as the picture is being taken? Maybe. His mouth is slightly open. Gough looks like he's listening to something Jason might be saying. Alejandra like she's stopped listening long ago. She looks like all she wants to do is take off her shoes. She's Spanish. How much English did she speak?

In front of Alejandra there are two small piles of empty plates, four and five plates respectively, and the remains of the cake, a thick creamy base on a huge shiny plinth, and small plates of stacked sandwiches with the crusts cut off. Next to the plinth you can see part of a bouquet, and on the extreme right of the photograph are some dessert bowls with what could be ice cream in them.

Where are Mum's wedding pictures? I've never seen them.

Jason was nineteen when he married Mum. Mum was so young, eighteen when she married and had Luke, that I forget he was too. They hadn't even been nineteen and eighteen for very long. Jason's birthday was the last day of March, three days after Mum's. They lived together first in Pimlico, then Maida Vale, Little Venice and finally Kingston. For somebody like Jason, a dreamer, a fast talker who felt entitled, London was the place to be.

During the week Mum never saw him. She'd wander all over the city with Luke in his pram. She didn't have any friends. She used the river - familiar shining water - to find her way.

But what do you know about it really? I never thought about them being in love.

Jason took her out at weekends. Up West to the 21 Club. Mum would sit dressed in her mink stole and long black gloves trying to look like she belonged. Jason was trying to get close to money, to be part of what was happening. Trying to get a connection. He didn't seem interested in the new scene that was happening and being made by people his own age – Soho places like the Scene Club in Ham Yard, or the Flamingo in Wardour Street. Jason liked clubs like the 21 where the crowd was older, established, a mixture of villains and society people. Everybody in black tie. Somebody might be on the lookout for a smart young kid like him. Somebody else might be weak and open to a con.

It must have worked sometimes. On his twenty-first birthday he flew Mum and half a dozen friends to Paris for the weekend. He put them up in the Hotel George V and paid for everybody. From somewhere he'd got a big score – or maybe his family gave him money for his twenty-first. Mum said they had money. They didn't think Jason should marry a poor girl like her. Does it say something good about him that he did anyway?

The next year, March 1964, on her twenty-first, Mum was alone in Kingston and pregnant with me. Kingston's the kind of place somebody like Jason would go to escape his creditors. You could reinvent yourself as someone respectable. A smart professional man with a young family. Keep up appearances until it was time to run.

Jason disappeared for good some time in April. The next day the bailiffs came and told Mum she had to get out.

I've imagined him leaving so many times.

I've written thousands of made-up words about it – always he drove away in an expensive car he hadn't paid for – but I don't know anything. Besides, I'm unreliable. Look at this picture. I can't tell you what Alejandra's dress is made of, or what the patterns on it are, they look like flowers, or what that bright border of what looks like tinsel is around her waist. What's in those two gift boxes on the table?

I was born in May, that's all I know. A month after he left.

It was always winter in the stories I wrote about Jason when I was young (1962–63 was a famous winter in London, one of the worst ever). I let him drive to the airport – the white car moving through an otherwise empty white landscape. At the airport he takes the new suitcase from the passenger seat. He leaves the car unlocked. I let him leave the piling snow and darkness behind (I was always thinking about mythology) and fly away to somewhere warm.

Either I wasn't real or I was too real.

Did he ever throw Luke in the air and catch him? Did he carry his son on his shoulders? Did he owe money? Did he just stop loving Mum?

In their last days together it was always dark and freezing. After Jason left the warm weather began again.

The more I look at the picture, the less Jason's jacket seems to fit.

Just because it's all I have, that doesn't mean the picture can tell me anything about my father. If I say that the note in his hand looks like a bill he can't pay or a promise he can't keep, I'm only saying that I made up my mind about him years before I saw his picture. I don't know anything. All I can do is make up stories.

And if you can't say who your father is what can you say about yourself?

I'm tired of thinking about all this.

Where did he go the night he left?

When I was twenty I went to Mozambique. The father of a girl I knew was living there. He got us the flights for free. I stayed for a month. War and famine had killed 40 per cent of the people. Only the European workers – from communist countries, mostly – had food. In Maputo, dogs and children scavenged in the red light of sunset. There was a curfew and it was difficult to leave the city.

When I came back I had nowhere to live. I saw Luke that night for the last time in two years, in a tacky nightclub above a pub. He was leaving for Australia the next day (or maybe Holland). Somebody took a picture. I'm very dark. My head is filled with the stories I'll write about Africa. I'm not unemployed and homeless. I'm just like Hemingway. I am drunk and dreaming and I look exactly like Jason in the only picture I have of him. My hair is cut the same way – short, in a side parting, but unruly in the same way as his. Same thick eyebrows. There is a band of flushed skin across my cheeks and nose, just like him. We look alike but it's more than this. Look how Jason seems apart from Gough and Alejandra, as if the conversation he's having with himself is more urgent and real than what's going on around him. Do you see? I know that look.

Vauxhall, London, 1988

Robin sweeps the white painted floor.

Dark wood shows through the whiteness in those places where the paint has blistered or worn away. Robin says I should sand off the paint and restore the true floor. She's right, it looks fake the way it is, but I like the ugly lightness.

I spread newspaper in front of the fireplace, ease out the grate, and dump the contents onto the paper. Make a heavy bundle of ash and pages and put it in a black rubbish bag. I'm trying to be careful, but I can't help dirtying the swept floor with cold ash and cigarette ends. Robin doesn't mind. She cleans up after me.

Robin's helping me move into a different room in the squat. A Saturday morning in May, 1988. Bonnington Square in Vauxhall, south London.

We can have fires, she said when she first saw the room.

Robin loves fires. At the farmhouse her father owns in the Auvergne, where we went together in March for the first time, we made a great ritual of making a fire in the evening, after we had been out collecting wood from the nearby forest. I'd chop wood, and together we'd build the fire. Make plans as it burned.

Robin's long hair is braided in a thick dark-blonde plait. She's wearing a soft red-checked shirt, canvas trousers and DMs. She has large dark eyes that are the first thing you notice about her when she's tired or upset. Seemingly becoming larger and limitlessly dark. So I can tell that Robin is not tired or upset this morning. She is happy to be helping me, and this morning, I have the sense to feel blessed by her love.

The room had been filthy. Maria, the dark, pretty girl who was in here before, never cleaned. We've used a roll of bin liners to bag up all the rubbish. There are saucepans grimy with old porridge. Dirty underwear. Hair and dust. Empty wine bottles with burnt-down candles stuck in the necks. Odd twists of burnt paper. Ruined books with handwriting over the pages. I only ever saw her when she was rushing to work. I wouldn't have guessed she lived like this.

Now the room is almost empty. There's the black-lacquered fireplace, a recess to the left with empty book-shelves that I've cleaned, a plain desk and chair in front of the bookshelves. A rolled-up futon we'll put down after I've washed the floor. My books are in boxes.

Maria's life went on outside this room. I'm planning on spending a lot of time here.

Robin has bought me flowers, luminous daffodils. I put the beer glass full of shining yellow flowers on my desk.

Robin has opened the sash window and is looking out onto the square. I join her, our heads side by side.

Look at the blossom, she says.

I'm twenty-three and Robin's twenty-two. For the past five years I've lived in different parts of London. I've spent a couple of summers at home, at the beach, but mostly I've been trying to make it in the city. I lived alone on a house-boat. Ash Island on the Thames. A cut-off world of dripping trees and moving water. The river rising and falling under-neath you as you slept. Woodsmoke and permanent damp. A cesspit in the woods. I lived with a tall, fair girl in a shared house in Dollis Hill that was so remote it did not feel like London at all. We split up, and before the squat I slept on a camp bed in the dining room of a restored Victorian house in Nunhead. There were working gas lamps in the room. I slept behind a Chinese screen. The man who owned the house had been in the navy years before with Robin's father. That's how I met Robin. The man was a good friend to me but he told me I was a destroyer and that I'd have to leave. I'd been drunk every night for a year.

I was drunk the first night I really paid attention to Robin. She wore a plain black dress, red tights and brown boots. Her long hair was brushed out, so that it fell over her shoulders, fair and shining. All of the light in the pub seemed concentrated in her hair.

This May morning feels like a new beginning.

Except I'm not fooled. It's Robin's love that's new, flooding me with sweet kindness and generosity I've done nothing to deserve. Like helping me clean up this room, my first real place.

There's the promise of a new kind of life. The farm-house, where there is a meadow that Robin says fills with wild flowers in the summer. We can go there any time, she says. We can walk in the meadow.

Blossom is soft aerial traffic.

The painted vans and travellers who were here in the winter have moved on.

Everywhere trees and flowers planted in the concrete are coming into life and colour – making the square of Victorian houses a soft space. Drifts of coral-pink blossom collect on the windowsill, fall to the pavement and to the gutters. Robin reaches out and catches blossom in her hands. Meanwhile I'm twenty-three for ever.

This is an end-of-terrace house. If I lean my head out the window and look left I can see across the playground to Vine Lodge – a stand-alone house filled day and night with musicians rehearsing and playing. There's always some-body in the square. There's no traffic. People stop and talk to each other. There's a man tending flowers. In different houses live carpenters, magicians, plumbers and singers.

Front doors are hand-painted. Ours says: *burst joy's grape on your palate fine.*

In the playground, a boy my age with dirty feet is walk-ing on a tightrope between two trees.

There are bike frames and wheels by the fence. I keep meaning to make a bike from the parts but I never do.

I take a drag of Robin's cigarette. She smokes Gitanes. I love the smell of them. Can I get away with smoking French cigarettes?

Every house here is squatted. Almost a hundred houses and over three hundred people. Free living ten minutes across the river from spiry castles of power.

The houses were opened up in the early 80s, when they were empty and abandoned, wiring stripped and plumbing dismantled and floors taken up. Houses with no roofs.

A handful of determined people worked hard to restore the houses. Now it's a village people come from all over the world to see. There is nowhere else like it – maybe not anywhere in the country.

After three months I still didn't really know anybody.

I'd heard that druids sometimes turned up at full moon, but I never saw one.

I've just drifted here.

The permanent community organizes. People go out into the city and forage for materials. There's a cafe where people volunteer to cook and serve. The food is free. It's true many of the squatters seem well off, middle class. Not people desperate for somewhere to live. But they are trying to build something.

For the travellers in decorated trucks and vans, the druids, the kids on the run from the only life that seems on offer, the square is a waypoint on seasonal journeys through an underground world of free festivals, solstice gatherings, camps in the woods. The promise of a safe harbour. Food and shelter. Addicts and users are cared for. There are lots of little children.

I take no part in meetings. I don't volunteer to help with the planting in the gardens or to help out in the cafe. I am always both present and dreaming.

The boy in the trees jumps down from his tightrope. He has fair curls, and I worry that Robin will think he's handsome. The boy looks up at me and Robin with blossom in our hair. He smiles.

Just moved in? he calls.

No, I've been here a while.

I haven't seen you around, he says. Got a cigarette?

Robin throws down a Gitane.

I could write about this place and you could photograph it, I say to Robin.

I'm going to photograph him, she says.

We brush blossom from each other and go back inside.

I take the bucket and Robin's wood-floor cleaner along the landing to the bathroom. It's dark in this part of the house and I step carefully where floorboards are missing.

Back in the room I put the bucket of hot scented water on the floor. Robin sits on the chair at my desk, by the typewriter and the bright yellow flowers. She hugs her knees, her feet in her sweet boots pulled up underneath her.

She smokes another Gitane and watches me.

I mop three-quarters of the floor and while it dries I sit in the chair and Robin sits in my lap. I play with her thick braid – make a moustache out of it, a beard. Robin laughs.

We have so much time.

When the floor is dry Robin helps me roll out the futon. We lie down. Robin stretches. She holds her arms out to me.

I'm dirty, I say.

So am I. It doesn't matter.

Later, at dusk, I tell Robin how I'm going to write in the mornings before work, and in the evenings I'll come up the hill to her place with chapters for her to read, and she'll have pictures to show me.

We look around the room. The desk and the flowers and typewriter and pile of clean paper.

The shelves are still empty.

Robin stands up to get dressed. She's going to the theatre with her mum.

She shows me a flat grey beach stone from Ver-sur-Mer.

Robin puts the stone on top of the pile of clean paper. For luck, she says.

When she's gone I open the boxes and take out the books and put them, one by one, on the shelves I've cleaned. I haven't seen these books in months, and I've missed them. I open books and sometimes postcards – from Luke, from all the faraway countries my brother's walked through – fall to the newly clean floor. I know what they say. I pick them up and put them inside different books.

I try out sequences of books on the shelf. There's a right arrangement and order and I need to find it.

Black Tickets, Love is a Dog From Hell, The Days Run Away Like Wild Horses Over the Hills, Death on Credit, Fires, Voices from the Moon. Hunger. The Grass Arena. The Outsiders, Rumble Fish. The Dharma Bums, On the Road. The Nick Adams Stories, The Sun Also Rises. History of the Russian Revolution (stolen from school. Unread). *Zen Mind, Beginner's Mind* and *Leaves of Grass* (both also unread). *Young Hearts Crying.*

Next to the typewriter I place a book – five years old now – called *Dirty Realism: New Writing from America.*

My love for certain writers is tribal – is it strange to say love? That year, Raymond Carver was the writer I loved more than any other – even Hemingway. The mystery in Carver's arrangement of plain words.

I open *Fires*, to the part where Carver says: 'For the details to be concrete and convey meaning, the language must be accurate and precisely given. The words can be so precise they may even sound flat, but they can still carry.'

I put paper in the machine and heavily, carefully, type: Girl, paper, stone, yellow flowers, book.

When I finish I sit looking at the words and smoking. In the summer I'd gone to hear Carver read. His friend Richard Ford was with him. What kind of man was Carver? It was long ago, and the room was packed.

Is it my imagination that the crowd was mostly young people? The chairs were all filled and we were sitting on the floor, at his feet. Except for Carver and maybe Ford, everybody was drinking. Red Stripe beer, I remember. Carver was elusive. He hung back, but although Ford was handsome as a movie star, anywhere Carver stood became the centre of the room. He wore a sports jacket, I'm sure of that. I thought he had a Slavic face – it was full and the winged shape of his dark eyebrows and the intensity in his eyes when you could catch a look at them somehow suggested this.

He was very shy and read poems in a stop-start, almost inaudible voice – despite the microphone. We leaned in to hear him. You had to really want to listen to what this man was going to tell you. And we did want to know, we all loved him. It was clear that what he knew had been hard won. Everything about how he was told you this. The way his eyes seemed to almost reconsider the words on the page before he said them. Besides, everybody in the room knew his story. I went to the bottom and didn't think I could go any lower, he said, but I got down there underneath the floorboards some place. Did he smoke even then? Yes, I think so. We all did. The place was full of smoke. He read the poem 'Alcohol', from *Fires*:

> *let her sleep*
> *in a proper bed. Let her*
> *fall in love with you and you*
> *with her and then . . . something: alcohol,*
> *a problem with alcohol, always alcohol –*
> *what you've really done*
> *and to someone else, the one*
> *you meant to love from the start.*

At the desk I opened *Fires* and read the poem again. Love is what Carver's people – who are all of us – are looking for though they don't always know it or find it. Love in a face you can't quite remember or horses that come to you out of the fog.

My sympathies are with these people, Carver said. People who have had the bottom fall out of things. I've known these people. I grew up with them.

I close the book. I leave the room and the house, and walk round to the pub in the warm spring evening, drifts of browning blossom eddying unnoticed at my feet.

I am passed out when Robin comes back. I wake to find her wrapped in a blanket, lighting twists of paper for the fire. Robin builds a little nest of sticks and she pushes the twists of paper inside and lights them. Some of the twists of paper escape and rise burning in the fireplace. She's patient. The little nest of sticks is on fire and she gently places a bigger piece of wood on the nest. The nest collapses, but the fire takes hold of the bigger piece of wood.

Robin is still nursing the fire when I fall asleep again.

Often that year I'd drink in the Queen Anne, a stripper's pub that stayed open late.

Sometimes I'd go there even when Robin was waiting for me in my room.

The only thought was to have more to drink. For the missing layer of skin it put on me.

I didn't care about the girls. I told myself I went there despite them, that the girls embarrassed me when really I was frightened by them.

The pub is across waste ground. Past dark action in derelict camps. The darkness moves – it's crawling with people. A brick or broken bottle in reach of every hand. Don't stop to piss. You're not even a tourist here.

The pub door and windows are boarded up with sheet-metal panels, but it's open, packed.

Inside, there's an imbalance of light. An overexposed pit where the girls strip. Starbursts of light come from the mirrors on every wall. The rest of the place is dark. The bar is at the back of the room, past the Chinese men in hats who play pool endlessly and never look at the girls. I buy beer and gulp it down. Buy more. I drink Tennent's Extra. Rocket fuel. I'm building a wall around myself with drink.

I light a cigarette, my last, and give a light to a man in an undone suit. His table is full of empty bottles, and there's a pile of 50p pieces in front of him. I notice his wedding ring.

A fat man in a wheelchair sits close to the pit.

In the end I have to look at the naked girl moving slowly to fast music.

Her skin is shark-belly white. An apparition in the darkness. Her face is still. Is she high? They say all the girls are high. She turns her back to us. Bends over and grabs her ankles. She sticks her arse into the grinning face of the man in the wheelchair, who wrinkles his nose like he's sniffing and then punches the air. Men cheer. Why's it me who feels naked and exposed?

When the girl, with wide-spaced grey eyes, dressed now in golden hot pants and a halter top, comes to me with an empty pint glass, I can smell the sweat on her.

I don't have a pimp, she says. A chipped tooth makes her lisp.

We fall in love. I save her. We are happy and have loads of kids.

What? I say.

The other girls all have pimps, but I'm not like that. I'm a proper dancer. I'm at Laban. Will you buy me a drink?

I black out. Wake up alone in my room, a full, open can of Tennent's on the floor beside me.

In the winter the house is often empty except for me, and the boy in the downstairs room who always keeps his door locked. Sometimes, when Robin is with her sisters, people come back from the pub with me.

Somebody says, Isn't there anything to eat?

The room is freezing. I begin to make a fire, banking it high.

A girl sits white and naked on the futon.

Aren't you cold? I say.

It is cold.

I'm freezing.

You don't eat, Somebody says. That's why you're cold.

Burning wood keeps falling out of the fireplace and I push it back in with my hands and force in more wood.

Don't put any more on.

I'm fucking *cold*.

I black out.

The room's on fire. There's nobody here. Running for water I nearly fall through where the floorboards are missing. I throw buckets of water on the fire. Open the window to the freezing cold. I fetch more water. I put the fire out. Fall back to sleep. In the morning I try to clean up. The wall above the fireplace is black and scorched. Pools of water on the floor. My hands are burnt. As best I can I bag up soaked masses of burnt paper and ruined books.

I stayed in the house for a few more weeks, until the boy who always kept his door locked killed himself with a shotgun he'd visited his father's house to retrieve.

I move in with Robin.

In the mornings she works in the studio she's made in the big bedroom. One year Robin made a series of pictures of men. The photographs she took of me when I was asleep and then awake, staring at her, were like pictures of two different people. There were pictures of fighters in the series – boxers – with smashed-in faces. The light-heavyweight champion, Dennis Andries, in his red robe, his massive dark fists wrapped in snowy tape. There were portraits of jazz musicians like Don Weller (with his sax) and the vibraphone player Ian Ballantine. These were musicians we went to hear play on Sunday afternoons at the Greyhound pub in Sydenham.

The flat smells of coffee and French cigarettes and the chemical scent of developer. I love to watch Robin making pictures. Her fair plait an anchoring rope as she works with tenderness and concentration.

We go to the farmhouse many times in the next seven years. We pick flowers in the meadow. Drive in the Auvergne mountains. Make fires at night. Drink. She nurses me when I become sick. We think of moving to the country. I cheat on Robin. We get dogs. I cheat on Robin. I stop drinking. I cheat on Robin.

10th December, London, 1995

I leave the top-floor flat filled with pictures. I walk down the tree-lined drive, past the empty swimming pool. I told Robin I was going into town to do some Christmas shopping, but I don't think she believed me. She was standing next to a large framed reproduction of a painting called *The Policeman's Daughter* when I said goodbye. The girl in the white dress, cleaning her father's huge jackboot, looks just like Robin. The same plaited hair, dark shadows around the eyes. The same ambiguous look that might be disgust or pride at what she's doing.

On Guy Fawkes Night, we had talked and talked, the first talk in months, me walking through all the rooms of the flat, Robin following, and finally we had sat with the dogs on our bed in our tiny bedroom, and held each other as the Catherine wheels and rockets blossomed silently outside. Rockets and fires burned all over the city.

Go? Robin cried. Why go?

I open my mouth to the cold winter air. It's one of those rare transparent London mornings when everything – the red rosehip berries on the trees, the cracked blue paint in the empty pool, a black cat whipping around the corner of the block – is so clear it almost hurts my eyes. Maybe it's just because it's early. I breathe in and out, hard. I watch my breath. I'm alive. I don't turn around to see if Robin is watching me from the high window.

The court of flats is next to Streatham bus garage, so that I can see the empty 159 bus that's going to take me into town, where I will meet Araba, leave the garage and come slowly to the stop where I wait.

I am wearing a wool-lined corduroy jacket, the wool the colour of a lion's mane. I love this jacket. It's thick and warm. I love the big collar that I can put up and hide myself in. I bought the jacket second-hand, years ago, with Robin. The shop I bought it in is closed now. Araba loves the jacket. It's soft. I wrap Araba in the lion's-mane wool lining and she snuggles into me. In the warmth of the bus – those low heaters that blow hot musty air at your ankles – the jacket smells of her, of cocoa butter and oils I do not yet know the name of. We are lovers now, since October, and I have already made the mistake of thinking she is mine, that she and her story belong to me.

Has Robin noticed the difference in the jacket she chose for me? Since October has she come close enough to notice that the jacket has a different scent? A different shape? That I wear this jacket every day? My heavy, steel-toecapped boots make a great clomping sound as I step onto the platform and bash up the stairs.

I sit at the front of the bus and try to read. I can always read but not this morning.

There's no traffic and no passengers. We're stopping for nobody as we rush towards my love.

Something from the book I can't read this morning – Jack Kerouac's *The Subterraneans*. Mardou Fox – she's the black girl the writer's in love with, and ties himself in knots over because he's scared of what his love means – he exoticizes her when he knows that's what he's doing, and talks over her even when he allows her to speak. He destroys their love in the end. Mardou says: What's in store for me in the direction I don't take?

Sitting under a heater outside the Bar Italia she wears a black wool dress, black tights, black steel-toecapped boots, black shawl. Her hair is pulled back – I've told her I like it that way – so that her cat's eyes and brown face – pale in winter, golden in the cafe lights – look faintly Asiatic.

I can't believe she is waiting for me (and she is not waiting for me, but for the person she believes I can become, the person I've told her I'll be and pretend to be when I am with her). She tells me I am gentle, peaceful. I am shining. Still I don't realize that she loves me. I am amazed she agrees to whatever I want to do. Later I understand that she withheld her intelligence, the wide, deep universe of all the things Araba knows, the languages she speaks – French and German, the instruments she plays – cello, piano, her lovers – men and women, her *faith*, the life she had already lived that made me seem like a child compared, so that she would not scare me away. In those first months she was trying to be what I wanted her to be. We were both pretending.

We go into a record shop and I buy *Somewhere* by Tony Bennett. I take her to look at paintings in the National Gallery. I had become used to looking at paintings. I try and tell her what they mean – all these paintings of white people – and she lets me and pretends to be interested. But of course she's tired. She loves the Christmas lights, the huge tree in Trafalgar Square.

The first cab won't take us to Brixton, and leaves us standing there. In the car we finally get, she closes her eyes. I hold her hand and watch her as Christmas lights float into the cab and across her face.

In bed Araba says: I'm glad we made love.

My dog – sweet India, a Labrador springer mix, black with four white feet like cauliflowers, a white star on her chest – jumps and puts her big white paws on my shoulders. I've been gone all day. India licks my face and hands. Her breath is hot and salty. I'm hardly in the door before Robin says: I know you're seeing somebody else.

Battersea Arts Centre, London, 1994

A black woman walks down the central staircase to the foyer of the building where I have recently begun working, holding hands with a little girl (her eight-year-old daughter, Lee – frizzed-out, lion-coloured hair). Light from a vast chandelier holds to the angles and plains of the woman's austere, lovely face. Big dark eyes made bigger with black eyeliner. A perfect, straight nose. Full lips. A tomboy figure. Sturdy, slim-waisted, small high breasts. It may just be that I will always want to look at her, but I think she expects to be looked at. There's a challenge in her smile. I know her name, Araba, and that she runs a theatre company with another woman. I haven't spoken to her – I've only been in the job a couple of weeks – and she's rehearsing a new play. I know this somehow.

The staircase is made from wide white marble steps, with rose-pink marble balusters.

Araba walks slowly down the staircase from the arched gallery where her office is. It's the opening night of a play she isn't in. I remember her in robes and gold. I stand in the open doorway of my bookshop, on a mosaic floor patterned with worker bees. Next to me is the sign that Robin made – an old Remington typewriter, and in the typewriter the opening paragraph of *A Farewell to Arms* (that I will one day read to Araba in bed).

In succession, the steps separate themselves from the

rest of the staircase and from the framing balustrade as Araba and her daughter reach them, so that each piece of white marble momentarily becomes a bright flying tile they ride on. Slowly they reach the ground in this way, as the bees rise to meet them.

The first play I saw Araba in was *Death Catches the Hunter*, by the Nigerian writer Biyi Bandele.

Come and see the play, my new friend says shyly, proudly.

Three characters: Emefa, a prophet. Saratu, who speaks in tongues, or who is an epileptic, or maybe both, and Peteru, Saratu's husband and Emefa's pianist, tell different versions of the same story. How Emefa becomes a prophet, and how he dies. He's eaten by a lion, but did he *mean* to be?

She played Saratu, of course, the woman who speaks in tongues.

Was she barefoot? No, this was a modern play. She wore flat sandals, a West-African print skirt and blouse, and a wrap for her hair.

The play begins.

Emefa says: 'Of my father, I do not know a thing. Depending on her mood – or mine – mother would often tell me that he was a bad man, or a good man. A kind man, or degenerate scum.'

Saratu tells the story differently: 'Take his father, for instance. He was a right monster, they said. They said he used to beat the prophet's mother to nonsense. He would come home drunk every night. They say the prophet really hated him. I mean, even his name proves it: Emefa . . . He doesn't have a surname. And I ask myself, could he have hated his father to that extent?'

Of course I thought they were talking about me. From the lighted stage Saratu was looking at me all night. I didn't know how the story would work out, but I didn't want her to kiss the actor who was playing her husband, or to kiss Emefa (she didn't).

I was dumbstruck by the ownership Araba claimed over space and attention.

In her overheated flat that night she told me she'd recently cut off the dreadlocks she'd worn for years. Was this the night I carried a warm, sleeping Lee up the stairs to the flat? Who did Lee think I was? My mum's already got a boyfriend, she said, the first time I tried to read her a story. Her fluffy hair tickling my arm. The lovely weight of her, the first child I'd carried.

I cut my locks off because I was hiding myself, Araba said. Do you understand?

Eastbourne was a conservative town. When I was a boy, the most visible political presence was that of the National Front. Their stickers – *Keep Sussex White, NF* – were everywhere. There was a junk shop where a dirty man sometimes had American comics. A black man walked through town one day, past the dirty man's shop where I was inside, looking for a superhero story I couldn't find. On a cold day the black man wore no coat. His hair needed cutting and he was talking to himself. His eyes said: I'm the only one of me in a world of you.

Look at that big nigger, the dirty man said.

A bookshop in Streatham. This was before I knew she existed.

The shop kept late hours. It was never very busy. It was a dead-end job. Nearly 10 p.m. Almost closing time. Across the road, stopped at the lights, is a red bus. The lights turn green. The bus doesn't move. There's no driver.

A white man and a black man are sitting on the bench seat by the open platform. The black man sits nearest the platform. Another black man is walking up and down the aisle waving what looks like a big knife. A machete.

You better call the cops, Ed, I say.

What is it?

See the bus? Tell them there's two black blokes, one of them armed, and they're holding another guy on the bus.

I hear him talking to somebody on the line.

They're on their way, Ed says, putting the phone down. They knew all about it. Ed's looking at me. He's a goofy redhead. Sweet. It was the first time, I think, that I had been admired by a younger man. Even though I've stopped writing Ed thinks I can tell him something about it. I'm twenty-eight. Ed's ten years younger and about to move to Los Angeles. What was I doing?

The police come. I hear them coming before I see them. The sirens. A car full. We are so close to what's happening, the window we watch through and are framed by is filled with electric blue light. Three of them, uniforms, get on the bus. The black man with the knife, the machete, hands it over. The policeman who takes it shakes the black man's hand. The two other uniforms stand over the white man. When the white man stands up, he's handcuffed. The police take him off the bus and push him into the back of the car. The policeman who shook the black man's hand and the other black man get off the bus. The policeman shakes the other black man's hand. The black man pushes his leather-looking cap to the back of his head, wipes his brow, puts his cap back on and walks to the front of the bus. He opens the cab door and climbs in. The driver starts the bus, the conductor pulls the rope and rings the bell. The policeman waves. The bus moves.

I become obsessed with swimming.

It started as a way to clear our heads on Sunday morning. Robin and her sister Tally and her partner Jan – we'd go together after a night's drinking. Jan had given me my first job in London – the bookshop in Chelsea where I'd heard Raymond Carver read (it was from Jan that I heard about Carver and the new American writers in the first place). For years the four of us did everything together and this was my family. Holidays to the house in the Auvergne. Sunday mornings Jan would drive us all to a pool in Chelsea. If it was just me and Robin we'd go down the road to the pool in Streatham. I'd swim until I felt well enough to start drinking again. Slowly I began to build up how far I could swim.

Then I stopped drinking and became very serious about swimming. I wasn't writing any more. I'd written a novel but it was no good. Every morning I swam a couple of thousand metres, and sometimes I swam again after work. Swimming gave a routine and pattern to each day that I couldn't stand to have disturbed. I'd cycle to Tooting Lido – a ninety-metre open-air pool in a park fifteen minutes from where Robin and I lived. A big expanse of water. I'd lived nearby for six years and never knew it was there. It was tucked in a corner of the park, almost like a glade, near to a stretch of road where I had sometimes seen prostitutes, all arses and heels, leaning in to the open windows of pulled-up cars late at night.

Midwater, you could not see where you'd come from or where you were going. I always thought it would be impossible for me to make the distance I had set. I always did. I wouldn't allow myself to swim any less. Each day the cold water was a renewal of the present. I'd think about Robin. How much I had loved her when we were kids seven years before. How I loved the home she had made for us. Then I'd think how I didn't have any choice about the way I felt about Araba.

The long straight swim to the wall. My stroke strong and steady. Turning to breathe, the bright, blurred sequence – red yellow blue green – of the painted cubicle doors. Some doors are open, others are closed. Sometimes I wished that the wall at the end of the pool wasn't there, that I could just keep going without having to turn back. Other times I was grateful for the familiar pattern.

Swimming made me feel strong and clean. I would sometimes be hit by blasts of pure ecstatic feeling. Maybe it was these shining signs of joy passing through me that

Araba was responding to. I didn't know what I was doing. Chasing after this woman I didn't know with a kid and who was pregnant again. I need to stop before it's too late.

But after swimming I would cycle to work across Clapham Common, and everything – the grass and trees, graffiti on the side of the old cafe, dogs running in the park, even their shit, was magical because I knew I would see her.

10th December, London, 1995

She doesn't know I'm coming. As sleet falls I stop by the usual phone box at the top of Brixton Hill. I lean my bike up against the box and open the door. For once, nobody has pissed in here. I can put the heavy bag down. Robin was crying. We both were. I just grabbed some things. I carry a black wetsuit draped over my shoulders. I'm scared one of the kids round here will steal my bike. I keep the door of the box open and twist my body so that I can hold the phone and the bike at the same time. I hear dogs barking. Is Robin running after me? Crying and running barefoot through the falling sleet, the dogs at her heels?

The lights of cars carrying people home in the late winter afternoon hit me in broken streams. I don't want to be seen and I let the door close and try and hide myself at the back of the box. I'm wet with sleet and it's cold and I blow on my red hands before I dial the number. It rings and rings. Maybe Araba's not there! What'll I do then? All my friends are Robin's friends. What I've left is home.

This tan, wool-lined corduroy jacket smells of Araba. The funk of her is on my face and hands even though the cold sleet and my tears and Robin's tears have worked to erase her. I close my eyes and press my head against cold glass and iron. In bed today Araba kissed me and her hair tickled my face. Her swelling belly pressed against me. The heat of her body. She looked at me solemnly.

What? I said.

I'm glad we made love, she said. Your face is so peaceful. It looks like my dream place.

How she said anything she wanted was something I was having to get used to. The way she talked to me made me wonder who I was. Who I could be.

In the darkness of her bedroom I was a new-formed knight. Thick velvet curtains separated us from any world.

Love, she said, that's what it was.

Will you call me an imperialist if I talk about her brown skin?

Araba is pregnant. The baby is not mine. It's Araba I want, and I would promise her anything. It's December, and the child is coming in the spring, but I can pretend it isn't happening (I've told Araba I want children). Her pregnancy makes her body fuller and even more desirable. My need for her is in my bones, and no matter how scared I am, she's where I'm going. For the possibility that I might become what she says I am. Am I the same person who ignored Robin's tears while I cried for myself? Why should I be rewarded?

I hope this is what you want, I say when she finally answers, because I've left her.

All along it's me who's forced this.

Come, she says.

I leave the blood-red box as car lights find me once more and I flinch and try to hide from the glare.

I get back on the bike and start down the hill again. At first I try to go slowly because the bag is heavy and I'm scared of the sleet going downhill, but more than this the precious black wetsuit is sliding around my shoulders (I knew you were really leaving, Robin told me later, because you took your wetsuit with you). I'm worried the arms or legs will flap and get caught in the spokes or the chain. If they do I'm a goner in this traffic and weather. In the end I think fuck it anyway and just freewheel down the hill, holding the wetsuit close with one hand as best I can. The increasing coldness I create as I pass through numbs me. Are these still tears?

It's a month on from Bonfire Night, more, but I can hear the clatter of fireworks exploding and see showers and arcs of lights between the tower blocks of the Holmewood Gardens estate. A kid rushes out from between parked cars, crossing the road dodging traffic as drivers slam on brakes and punch horns.

A bigger kid chases him, holding a foot-long rocket waist-high. I can hear the rocket sizzling, see sparks showering to the ground. I see the kid fire the rocket as I swoosh wetly by, hear it thump and bang against a parked car. He shouts at me but I don't hear what he says, there's just a voice disappearing behind me in the sleet as I accelerate crazily down the hill, to where I'm headed.

Brixton, London, 26th March 1996

Araba wakes me gently.

The baby's coming, she says.

It's so dark I can only just make out her face, the far-away lights in her eyes, her swollen lips. I don't know who or where I am. It's the middle of night, later.

Are you OK?

The baby was a week overdue. I didn't mind. If Araba was scared (how she must have been) she didn't show it to me. But she was impatient of course. I was happy to wait. For that week we seemed to exist apart from anything going on around us. That morning – bright, clear – Araba was desperate to get out, and we had been walking in Covent Garden. In a skate shop in Neal's Yard, Araba bought us matching pairs of huge, chunky skateboarding shoes. Maybe they just looked so comfortable, they had these bumper soles, and her feet had been hurting for months now and maybe the shoes would help.

We came back to the flat with the two boxes of stupid shoes. I hardly wore mine, but Araba really did like them. Araba rang the midwife. Araba boiled the kettle.

The midwife said to drink some parsley tea.

I'll make it, sit down.

Araba made the tea and drank the whole pot.

We went to bed early. Carefully made love. The baby kicked like crazy.

She woke me gently.

Sometimes when we were out together and people saw that Araba was pregnant, they would smile at us. Because of this I sometimes had to get away for a day or two but I always went back, and pretended I went away because of something else (she wasn't fooled).

I get out of Araba's bed a stranger. I don't know myself In the bathroom the citronella plant is out of control. I want to cut it back but it's not mine. It's crazy to be thinking like this when Araba's about to have her baby.

The midwife arrives. I remember nothing at all about her. Also Araba's friend and ex-girlfriend Jennifer. Araba needs a friend, another woman, somebody who really knows her and will look after Lee. Jennifer – serene, wrapped dreadlocks, low voice – lights lamps and sets out tea lights and aromatic oil burners throughout the flat. Small points of candlelight partly illuminate Jennifer's many bracelets, and the many photographs of Araba's family – the men and women, black and white, dead and alive, all unknown to me, who look down from her walls. Beyond the lights are graduated fields of darkness and shadow. I'm at the edge, the limit of the light.

Araba's face in the lamplight is very still and withheld and far away and then contorted when her contractions come. Araba gives deep moans and growls rising in pitch to an uncontainable yell. I want the noise to stop. Every thought for myself is shameful.

I'm sure I thought of Araba. How close by was I, anyway? Was I with her all the time?

Then, suddenly – really, in a *rush*, we will all remember how quickly Jay was born – here's the baby. I'm the first person she sees, this new being! She's red and bloody, of course, with a shock of thick black hair.

I can feel myself smiling. I'm so glad Araba's all right, and at the same time I feel such terror. How can I be here for the birth of another man's child? Holding the baby – who's making little snuffling noises, like a tiny bear – Araba says: We have a baby. Maybe she said, We have our baby.

Her upturned face in the peach-coloured lamplight is full of love and hope. It breaks my heart to think how great a distance there is between us.

I've made promises I cannot keep.

This baby is not mine.

Brixton, London, 1998

The children sleep downstairs, at the back of this badly made house. The two bedrooms are darkened and hushed by heavy velvet curtains. Lee's room is pitch-black, her window is small, and her curtain smothers all light, but sodium-yellow security lights bleed into Jay and Rose's bedroom from outside, so that when I go to Rose – who's woken, she's crying and wants changing and feeding – a faint golden frame seems to hang and float in the darkness.

I haven't remembered to ask Jay if she's ever noticed or thought about the floating frame of light. Probably she hasn't, not because she's only two and a half, but because when she can't sleep she doesn't stay in her cot. And anyway the window, and the curtain, are behind her headboard, so she wouldn't be able to see it unless she switched ends, which she does sometimes, either deliberately or in her broken sleep. At other times when she can't sleep Jay climbs out of her cot and comes up the stairs to our bed room, A red hippo dangling from her mouth. She stands by the bed and stares at me. Not moving or hardly making a sound. Eventually Jay's not moving hardly making a sound presence wakes me up.

Jay stands absolutely still staring at me. I wake up. I'm always frightened at first. Jay's wild hair is all puffed up. She wears a red onesie that smells of rice milk. In the moment I realize Jay is there, Araba wakes up and talks softly to her and brings her into the bed with us. I have to reassemble myself. Recognize who Jay is and what my relationship is to her. Araba is Jay's mum the second she opens her eyes. Somehow I always knew when Jay was standing silently and not moving by the bed before I woke up. Then I woke up and it would be true. After a few times Jay must have known I didn't like her coming up the stairs and standing by the bed and staring at me until I woke up. Did that make her scared of me? Jay wanted her mum, of course.

I didn't want Jay in the bed. I wanted the bed to be for me and Araba.

Rose is in my arms. Jay's playing with her bricks on the wood floor. Rose has finished the rice milk I heated up for her. I watch my daughters through a lemon gauze of October light that feels precious and temporary. The walls and doors of this house offer no protection.

If you slam the door, as Araba did this morning when she was leaving with Lee, the house shakes for a long time afterwards. There's a fist-sized hole in the bathroom door (hollow, made of thin board) from another fight. I punched it when Araba wouldn't open the door.

It no longer matters who starts the arguments. The pattern is set.

The wood floor floats in the light that washes over the baby's face and my arm that holds the bottle. Rose's eyes are closed. The dark lashes are impossibly long. She is clean and warm. She opens her eyes. They are enormous and deep. She stares at me. What's she seeing? Whatever it is, it's OK for her to shut her eyes again and return to dreamy suspension in my arms. She sighs and I pay attention. I lean in to smell her. Often a sigh comes after she's filled her nappy, but it's fine this time. I breathe in the warm biscuit scent of her head.

My Rose.

Jay was crying earlier but she's all right now. She has her own bottle of rice milk – as usual she's almost completely chewed through the teat and the bottle's hanging out of her mouth. She crawls over to me, the rich mass of her hair wobbling. Something about the material – some kind of plastic – used to pad the feet of her onesie makes her crackle softly as she pushes off the floor. No, it's her nappy! Maybe that's what wakes me up at night.

Jay loves me to play with her. I haven't played with anybody since I was a kid. Jay loves to wrestle and fight and to climb on me and for me to carry her on my shoulders.

She really loves it when I throw her up in the air and catch her. When I throw her up, and she comes falling into my arms, I concentrate on the laughing child rising and falling, trusting me to catch her, which I always do. I notice the changing weight of her in my arms.

It's hard to love.

Lee's at school. She couldn't wait to get out of the house this morning. I try and be a friend to her. She sees her dad at weekends – there's no question of trying to take his place. Still, I try and take her side when she fights with him – even when she fights with Araba.

Secretly she wants to travel when she's older. I tell her, go ahead. She's thirteen. Everything's changed for her. Lee had Araba to herself and now here I am – and two baby sisters! – taking up all the space and time that was once hers. It's true I don't think about her enough.

Later I'll make her bed. She's always really pleased when I do that and sometimes writes a sweet note to tell me.

I have to stop shouting at everybody.

As she sleeps, I trace the high arch of Rose's soft, tiny foot. She has my feet. Her eyes and nose and legs and wide shoulders are mine. What else?

Dadda.

Jay holds my leg and pulls herself up.

Hello Bear.

Jay looks at her sister. Rose's eyelids flutter and she makes a kind of chirping sound.

Oh, Jay says, in her little sing-song voice. She looks at me. Rose made a funny noise, she says.

She did. Like a little bird. What noise do birds make?

Cheep cheep.

Good Bear.

Jay drops down and crawls away again, saying cheep, cheep.

I look down at Rose. I worry that if I give Rose too much love I'm not loving Jay enough.

You only love Rose, Araba shouted this morning. You didn't live with us until Rose was born and you didn't come until I was in labour and I had to call Steve to come and get you because you don't have a phone. Fuck! She slammed the door.

—

Jay comes back with a story book – *Where The Wild Things Are.*

Story, she says.

She loves stories about monsters.

Where's Hippo? I say.

Hippo is a red bean-bag toy, dense and crunchy. He has ears and a little tail that Jay loves to chew on, and mostly this is how she carries him, chewing on an ear so that Hippo dangles from her mouth. When she's drinking her rice milk, like now, she has to take Hippo out of her mouth and put him down. Because she is never still, sometimes she forgets where she's put him and then Hippo is lost and everybody who's here has to look for him. Araba has some extra hippos hidden away, but Jay isn't fooled. They are too red and clean. The real Hippo has a burn mark on his bum. Jay won't sleep without him. She crawls over to her box of bricks. Reaches in and pulls out Hippo. She holds him up by a red ear.

Hippo! I say.

She laughs and crawls back to me and climbs up onto the sofa.

Story, she says.

As I read the story about the little boy meeting the monster that lives inside him, before returning to love, my monster, the one that lives inside me, is quiet. For once not raging and filling my head with his noise. Making me punch holes in the walls. I'm surprised the monster is quiet. When I'm around the kids he's usually busy, telling me that I'll be a shit dad, like I was a shit kid and am a shit man.

This strange October peace is bathed in fragile light. The monster is quiet but I know how much danger we are in. Will I hit Araba the next time she says something I don't want to hear?

Dadda.

Jay's looking at me. I realize the book is open in my lap. Jay's trying to lift my heavy hands from it so that she can turn the page and see what happens next.

Sorry Bear, I say, and lift my hands.

St Paul's, London, 1999

He's a cunt, Dale told the giant teenage twins who worked with us. But I like him. Dale liked me because I was good at smashing things that he told me to smash, or hod-carrying huge loads of bricks until the numbing pain spread across my shoulders and down my spine in a way that was almost comforting. But I was hopeless at any kind of job I had to build or make, and that's one reason Dale called me a cunt.

After Araba threw me out, I moved around a lot, sleeping on floors. The only work I could find was as a day labourer. Each night I spent my wages in the pub. In the morning I'd try to work out how to get to the site from wherever I'd ended up.

You've got to stop fucking boozing, Dale said.

I'm going to Mexico.

I should fucking think so, Dale said.

Dale had the kind of round white face, smudged like an unwashed dinner plate, that you see everywhere in England – in the pub, at the football or the curry house – and don't give a second thought to. These were the last days of the job – a ten-floor new build for a music company, just around the corner from St Paul's.

One Monday morning near the end Dale wasn't on the gate when I got to work. I couldn't remember him ever not being there. Nobody could tell me where he was, not even the twins. I was feeling bad, weak and feverish. I went up to the tenth floor and found a dark corner and lay down. I'd seen my girls on the Sunday. My daughters both had new toys they wanted to show me.

We sat in the communal garden. I told the kids where I was going and why. I'm not sure how much they understood. Jay was three and Rose was two. They had cried the day I left, but that was because I was screaming and smashing furniture. Now they clung to me as we sat on the bench. They kissed my unshaven face and listened to me lie as I told them that I would be back soon. I looked into their clear, brown faces, trying to remember. Their dark eyes reflected my red and swollen face. Their sing-song voices were sharp blades. Two dark figures watched us from the kitchen. It could have been Lee with Araba, but she went to her Dad's on the weekends.

One night, drunk and high, I'd blacked out in the street in Brixton. One second I wasn't there and then I was. When I came round I had broken ribs and a busted-up face, one eye punched shut. What had I said or done to get a beating? I rang Araba that night from where I was staying.

Can I see you (I never stopped thinking she was mine)?

I'm with someone, she said. I knew who she was with, I had attacked him in the street once, in front of Araba and Lee.

Dale was back that afternoon. He found me and kicked me awake.

The fucking matter with you? he said.

Nothing.

You look fucking terrible, he said, lighting a B & H. What's the fucking matter?

Nothing.

Come on, he said, handing me a 10lb sledgehammer, the shitter in the basement.

At the start of the job the carpenters had put up a toilet block made of plasterboard and plywood. There were half a dozen stalls and a trough. At its busiest there were hundreds of men on site. There was no ventilation. It was impossible to say how many thousands of men had used the toilet. The wood under the trough was soaked with piss. You could smell the place from a long way away.

Carrying sledgehammers we walked down the steep, winding slipway that Dale and I had mixed and put down all the cement for in a single shift, just the two of us. The toilet block stood in the middle of what would be the building's car park.

The basement was dark but the toilet block was under a row of bright strip lights, one of which was faulty, and buzzed and flickered. Somebody had already taken the doors off the stalls and the toilets had been unplumbed. The waste pipes were caked with dried and not so dried shit.

Smash it up, Dale said.

Go on you cunt! Fucking smash it!

I lifted the sledgehammer above my head and swung it feebly at the plasterboard wall, not even breaking the skin.

Dale waded over with his own hammer.

Fuck's sake!

He swung the hammer and punched out a massive hole in the plasterboard. He pulled the hammer free and swung again, and more plasterboard and dust and shit went flying everywhere. He swung at a toilet bowl and it exploded in a shower of shit and dirty porcelain. Shit splashed his face and he laughed. Ha ha ha! You cunt, he said, and swung again.

Dale was swinging his hammer and laughing and crying. Sweat and tears and gob flying off him. Then I was crying and swinging my hammer like it weighed nothing, punching through the wooden frame and the walls and ceiling. Shit all over me. When it was done we stood sweating and stinking, breathing hard under the light that had stopped flickering and now burnt brightly. It wasn't until we were in the pub that he told me he'd buried his dad that morning.

San Augustinillo, Mexico, 1999

Wim comes from his cabin with the mescal. Why does everything feel so predetermined?

Beyond the light of this driftwood fire the Pacific is a dark moving permanence. Onshore winds rattle the crowns of the high palms all along the sweep of the beach.

Ya viene una tormenta, Dolores said.

Lizards, dogs and wild pigs look for shelter. My feet are buried in sand.

Dolores is inside her place now, sleeping with the two little kids – Jesus and Maria – who look exactly like her. Small, dark, with neat, bobbed black hair. The children are interested in the travellers. The girl likes to help Dolores make the food – the fish, rice and beans – she sells to us. The boy especially loves to go fishing with Wim.

Was it this morning I sat in the back of the camioneta travelling on Highway 175 to Pochutla?

The pick-up full of men and women going to market. At the post office I put the letter in the mailbox. I have a poste restante address but there are no letters for me. At the bank I queue to cash my last traveller's cheque. I buy chocolate and apple cinnamon empanadas at the bakery. The air in Pochutla is cloudy with granular dust. I wait for another camioneta to bring me back to this almost empty, half-moon-shaped beach between the mountains and the ocean. San Augustinillo, on the Pacific coast of Mexico. The mountains are the Sierra Madre del Sur.

I hope Araba waits until she's alone before she reads the letter to the kids. I give the bag of sweet empanadas to Dolores. Para los niños. Dolores takes the empanadas but won't speak to me.

Yesterday I went fishing with my friend Faron. Faron is an American. He has long grey hair and a grey beard, and he wears a big hat with a feather in it. We borrowed the boat from Wim. Wim is a Dutchman who lives here, in a little cabin on the beach. Wim is friends with Dolores. Dolores is the lady who runs the place where I live. She has the children I told you about. The ones about your age. Faron brought Rebel in the boat. Rebel is a big yellow dog.

Wim left the campfire a while ago – in the middle of a story Faron was telling – and went into his cabin. I know he's coming back, and I know he'll have the mescal with him.

And so, Faron says, they take me out of the county jail, and this cop finally gets me into this van to go to court after me resisting all this time, man, and as this thing is *accelerating* I have to throw up, I just have to, and this *ball* of vomit goes straight into the cop's face.

Faron is a source for the stoned kids sitting at the fire with us, his stories are scripture. I've drifted along with him for three months.

I got a son your age, he said when we first met. He's studying law.

Where is he?

He's somewhere in Texas with his mother, I think.

You ever have a dog, Faron? I say to him.

An Argentinian kid – the one with the dreadlocked girl-friend – passes Faron a joint and he sucks on it and passes it to me.

Dogs? Sure I've had lots of dogs. Had a good dog when I was farming weed in Colorado.

What happened?

I had to leave him behind, man, you know how it is.

Sometimes, like now, the way I can look down and see myself sitting by this driftwood fire on the beach, in the lee of Dolores's place, I feel I'm already remembering being here. I do not look like myself. I've lost a lot of weight. I'm very dark.

Once, Rebel jumped into the sea for a swim and we had to pull him back into the boat. Rebel shook water all over me and Faron laughed. We saw a sea snake!

Mostly though, I feel like I've been here for ever, like Wim, and that what I'm looking at, as tin-coloured clouds race across the moon, and the lean, self-involved man who is me and who is not me looks up to notice this, is a man whose heart is not here, but far away, and this is why I don't recognize myself. I am turned to stone by too much thinking.

Were those vultures I saw riding darkly on thermals above the Sierra Madre?

Coming back from the hillside posada this afternoon I walked in the foothills of the mountain not knowing what I was looking at. Was this mesquite, or sagebrush? That wild pig I thought I saw crossing the arroyo is not a pig but a javelina.

The sea snake was yellow and black and swam right next to the boat. Rebel barked at it. It was good to be out on the sea. We caught a lot of fish called red snappers, and that night we cooked them all on a fire and everybody on the beach ate some. Rebel had two!

You think old Wim is still sore at us? Faron says in a low voice.

I expect so.

What about you? You mad at having to tow us all that way?

You can't swim, that's what you said.

That's right man, I can't!

The light goes off in Wim's cabin, and I hear and then see his dark, stretched outline coming across the beach. He sits down by the fire. Tall and slim with just the first signs of slackness in his arm and chest muscles. Jet-black hair that is always neatly barbered. He's clean shaven. Wim is twenty years older than all of us who are living at the beach, except Faron.

It's all right, he says to me, drink some mescal.

The bottle goes around the campfire. Is drunk from and held up to the light.

I took the engine into Puerto Angel, Wim says. There's nobody here who can fix it. I don't know what it's going to cost.

I'd like to help, Faron says, but like I said it was an accident. I can't afford to pay for an engine that was fixing to break any time. There's a saying in Mexico, man: What cannot be remedied must be endured. I've only got the clothes on my back.

It's how you wear them Faron, Wim says.

I'm starting a job tomorrow. I'm helping build a new floor in a guest house – a posada in Spanish – on a hillside just outside this village where I live. I'm going to work there for about three weeks and then I'm coming home. I know Mumma told you I said I'd be staying here maybe for good, but I've decided to come home.

The storm comes in the small hours. I was dreaming I was at sea. When I wake the wind is ripping into the palms above my head. Huge rollers smash onto the shore. In my hammock I swing in the wind.

Wim appears out of the dark, haloed by stars. He hands me a blanket.

Thanks.

Maybe you should move higher up the beach. He has to shout over the wind. Faron's already inside, he says.

Faron's hammock is empty.

I let him sleep in my place, Wim says.

I'm all right here.

Wim starts to walk away.

Wim, I say.

He comes back. Bends down close to me so I don't have to shout. Holds the hammock to stop it rocking.

We should never have taken her out, I say. I thought Faron knew how to handle a boat.

Well, thanks for bringing her back. It was a long swim.

It wasn't that far.

The boat isn't mine, Wim says. It belongs to Dolores. Without it Jesus and me can't catch fish – that's all she really has here to sell – fish and rice and beans. That's all any of us have. We can go out with somebody else for a while, but I'd have to give them something.

The money from Pochutla is in an envelope.

Here, I say, please accept this.

Wim opens the envelope and looks at the money inside.

You think you can just buy us?

I don't know what else to do.

Wim puts the envelope in his shorts pocket.

I'll tell Dolores, he says.

Thanks for the blanket.

Sure you don't want to come in?

I'm all right. It's nearly blown itself out.

In the early morning the women of the village – including Dolores – are sweeping the street. The women walk in a line, talking and laughing, wearing rebozos to keep the dust from their hair.

Jesus and Maria are running on the beach, shouting and pointing out to sea. The ocean is endlessly bright. Grey whales, two adults and a calf, surface in light, expelling great clouds of air and spray. I stand and watch the family of whales, then walk on up the street towards work.

Brockwell Park, Brixton, London, 2004

Below me, the quince light of the low morning sun pops and sparkles on the water's surface. I put my sunglasses back on, and the light softens once more to honey. Moving figures – swimmers, sunbathers, little kids at the poolside – are transformed. Through my dark lenses at this early hour, I allow all figures to be androgynous.

Then a girl in a sheer bikini goes by, all insistent curves, and bang! here comes the heat.

Now the water's little crests and hollows are honey-combed with light, the pool alive with these movements of changing colour as though the concrete walls struggle to contain some bright, new-becoming life. I want to tip this pool – I'm a superhero, an ant-size figure holding the giant pool upended, balanced on my tiny hand – and pour its brightness out over the world.

The woman who only has one summer dress – washed-out, lilac, with a ragged hem – is here with her son again. The boy is eight or so, black-haired, Spanish-looking, grave, dressed always in black shorts. Both of them are barefoot. They have no towels or food. Nothing to drink. The boy has a T-shirt, always the same one, plain, a worn dark olive colour, that he uses as a towel and that his mother spreads out to dry while he's swimming. No flab or pose on this kid. He never smiles, is stone-faced all the time. His fore-arms are corded with veins and his hands, impossibly, are thick as a labourer's. The woman never swims, just sits watching the boy and hugging her knees. I can't figure them out. What their life together is like. I only assume they are mother and son. Maybe she found the boy, and made him the king of her small rooms.

Vigilance by itself will not make you a good lifeguard but it's the first requirement.

A fifty-metre open-air swimming pool in Brockwell Park, south London. It's either the *leedo* or the *lydo* depending where you come from. For me it's the *lydo*.

I spoke to my girls last night. They're on holiday – with Araba and her father and stepmother in the West Country. When they're away I sometimes feel like I did in the year when I did not live under the same roof as them. Often I remember Mexico as a dreamed place, where I was a ghost-man wandering. The only thing sharp and real was how it felt to be without my children. Did Jason ever feel that way? That what really mattered in his life was taking place beyond his sight and knowledge? Maybe all he felt was freedom, and I did feel freedom, all those months camped out under the moon and the stars, but too much of it made me sick.

The kids had grown so much!

You're too thin, Araba said when she saw me after I got home.

Now we work towards a gentler love.

With the sun behind them, the devoted pair of mallard ducks that have made the pool their home come flying over the shallow-end wall together. From here – the deep end – I can't tell the male from the female. They're just dark forms. Using wide, outstretched wings for drag, and pushing webbed feet out in front of them, the birds aquaplane across the water's surface and coast gently to a stop just below me. Now I can tell them apart. The male duck's emerald head shines in the morning.

I tap my wedding ring against the chair's tubular arm, rub the growing callus on the skin below the ring with my thumb.

Last night, Araba told me that some money had been taken from her purse. She thinks it was Jay.

Did you talk to her?

Of course, Araba said. Her voice recovers its childhood music whenever she goes home.

And?

She said it wasn't her.

This high chair is hot against my thighs and bare back. A bolted plate fixes it to a diving board. The bolts are copper-red with rust and one has come loose. The chair tilts with a chunking sound whenever I shift my weight. Blue paint from the chair and the board has blistered, and tiny blue flakes stick and glisten in the sun oil on my skin.

Here's a kid, a small, dark boy making haphazard progress through the water towards me. I lean forward, watching hard, and the bright silver charm of my whistle swings out and back repeatedly, the arc of each swing diminishing until the hot tin comes to rest against my chest that feels scorched and hollow inside. I sit with my hands resting gently – hardly resting at all – on my thighs, my body made slippery and somehow insubstantial and absent by the mixture of oil and salt and water it's coated in. I do not trust the solidity of my body enough to lean my elbows on my thighs and rest my chin on the heels of my hands. If I do so all these various parts of myself will slide from each other and fall down into the water.

Outside, crowds gather at the gates. I look up at the sun. It's going to be a burner.

I reach beneath the chair, find my water bottle, and drink. My insides cool as the water goes down. I take off my hat and pour cold water on my head. I come back to myself, put my hat back on. I do not stop looking at the water. I am looking for movement that isn't right – for breaks in the familiar patterns.

The kid swims face down in the water, close to the safety rail, kicking his legs, his body wriggling, lifting his head to breathe. His eyes are closed and he rubs at them before opening them and looking around to see where he is. He's holding on to the safety rail. He looks up at me. I smile at him. What does he see when he looks up?

A troop of three little girls with shining eyes, all around six years old, arms and legs working furiously under the water, come swimming up to me. Giggling, trying to hold their breath and keep their heads out of the water all at the same time. The leader, a biscuit-coloured girl with an Andean face and her black hair in tight buns and a severe centre parting, grabs for my foot. The black bands that hold the little girl's hair in place have yellow jaguar heads on them. All the girls wear bright bikinis. Rose has the same costume.

Where's Rose? the black-haired girl says, we swam all the way to ask you. We can't find her.

I jump down from the chair and stand at the poolside.

Hello Tia, you little bean. Hi Ooshi, hello Amber.

The girls all live in the same block as us.

Where's Rose! the girls all shout at once.

Ooshi, a white girl with a runny nose, grabs the rail. Her cheeks have red spots on them.

Amber, black, slender, reaches for Ooshi, who puts her arm around her waist.

Your cheek's hot, Ooshi, Amber says, have some water darling, it will cool you down.

She splashes Ooshi and then kisses her cheek.

Where's Rose? Tia says.

She's on holiday with her mum.

Where?

To the countryside to visit her grandad.

Rose has gone on holiday! Tia shouts.

Traitor! shout Ooshi and Amber.

And do you even know where she's gone to? Tia says.

Where?

To the countryside!

Death to the traitor Rosie! all three girls shout at once.

It's so unfair, Ooshi says, and sneezes. A thick bubble of lime-coloured snot comes out of her nose.

Oh my God Ooshi, Tia says, get rid of your snot girlfriend! Eeeurgh!

Oh my God, Amber says.

We're not really going to kill Rosie, Tia says.

I know.

But she is a traitor. We all *swore* we'd come on the last day and she *lied*.

She couldn't help it sweetie.

That sucks so much I can't even tell you, Tia says.

They're coming back today. Rose's mum will bring her if they get back in time.

Yay! Push me under.

I pretend to push down on the girl's tar-dark head and Tia goes under. She duck-dives and her little brown feet appear above the surface for an instant. I watch her straightening in the water. The small brown girl heads for the bottom of the pool, arms by her side, bubbles streaming from her. I see her reach out and touch the bottom and then arch her back and kick up, rising with her head back and eyes closed, sunlight hitting her face and chest as she nears the surface.

Did you see me? she says.

Yes, I say, I told you it would be easy by the end of the summer.

Did you teach Rose how?

Of course.

OK, she says, gotta go. Come on guys.

As the girls began to swim away furiously, Tia shouts: See ya! Wouldn't wanna be ya!

I climb back in my chair. I am conscious of the noise behind me. All the different tribes and gangs of kids from the area are gathered behind this chair. The lido is a neutral space. Any disputes are left outside. But there's still a lot of shouting and showing off. There are groups of kids from different estates in Brixton, Tulse Hill, Streatham, Stockwell. Challenging us is part of their day.

At the start of my first season, I asked Stranger what I

should do if there was trouble. Not in the water, on the poolside.

I've worked here for years at the front, at the gate meeting all the people, Stranger said. The kids, boys, girls, everybody, I meet them. Who is their mother and their father. I know the troublemakers; I know the good-behaving kids; I know everybody. Sometimes I have to ban them.

OK.

It's not nice banning kids but sometimes you have to do it in order for them to learn and have some discipline. One thing we have to maintain here is discipline. We don't mind about rude boys, but when you come here you follow the law, and if you don't you get a ban, simple.

OK.

You are the law. You have a hat?

No.

You must have a hat.

Now I'm in charge of the lifeguards. I've watched a lot of these kids grow up. I taught Rose and Jay to swim here.

The pool is a repository of light and movement. Beyond the red-brick walls and past the golden flags posted on the roof – the flags slack for weeks now in the hot windless air – is the burnt park where yesterday I saw a white dog, floating on the granular dust cloud it had made. The sun has split the hard, asphalted surfaces of the tennis courts.

Rose has spent most of the summer here. She comes with me and we go home together. Everybody is happy to see her. She spends hours in the water, looking for treasure.

Rose is brown, sturdy, in her head is a vision of the world as it should be. We eat lunch together and she talks and talks.

Jay will only swim on the hottest days but she gets cold too quickly – there's no fat on her body – to really enjoy it. Jay needs to run, she's not one for dreaming in the sun, like me and Rose. So mostly she's at home, or in the park, playing football with her mates – more kids from our block – Che, Krystian and Tyreese. She's such a tomboy.

Maybe just be careful not to leave your purse out, I said to Araba.

School starts tomorrow, she said.

I know.

Jay won't say why she hates school so much. Near the end of the long summer holiday is the worst time. She becomes sullen, and shouts at her mother. This is not the first time money has gone missing. I try not to worry too much. What kid doesn't hate school? After a while things seem to settle down. Mostly when I go to pick her up she seems happy – always she is changed into her tracksuit bottoms and is playing football with her friends. She comes running into my arms when she sees me. It's true it's almost impossible to get her to do her homework, and I worry about what will happen when she goes to big school.

A thousand piercings flash in the sunlight. Thick ranks of kids dive, jump, bomb, backflip and somersault into the water. Everybody shouts at once. Boys pull girls in. Girls pull boys in. Climbing out, the girls unstick bikinis from their bums, adjust tiny triangles of soaked material over their breasts. The boys all grab their crotches, squeeze water from their shorts. Shake their heads so that a fine mist seems to hang permanently in the air. All heroes to themselves.

The same dark boy is back out in deep water. He's doggy-paddling out of his depth in the centre of the pool. I whistle at him again. The boy looks up. I point at the safety rail that runs down the side of the pool. I should have seen him before he got out there again.

The dark boy tries to nod, and his head goes under. I stand up. The boy surfaces, embarrassed, waves and begins to swim awkwardly to the side. The water's so thick with people the boy has to sometimes tread water to let somebody pass. I give the boy the thumbs up and sit back down in my chair.

Stranger is a large sleepy-looking dog-faced man. He's got fourteen kids. On a given day there's a handful of them here. He's got the oldest couple on the payroll. Before I knew him I'd sometimes seen him cycling slowly around Brixton on a kid's too-small BMX bike, wearing basket-weave shoes, his knees at perfect right angles. Often he'd have a kid on the back pegs and another riding on the frame in front.

A pair of upturned black feet attached to long, narrow black legs periscope above the surface. A ladybird walks – an intense movement of red and black – along the tubular arm of my chair. I put my hand out and the ladybird walks up on to it and then opens its wings and flies away.

A small hand grips my foot.

Hey bruv. Bruv! Can I jump off your board?

Sorry, it's not for diving from.

'Low it man! It's not your pool bruv.

Yes it is.

Bloodclaat battyman! the kid shouts, jumps and grabs the side of the board, swings hard, lets go and somersaults into the water.

I laugh.

In the chair to my right Thanmai sits upright and straight-backed, hands palm-up on the arm rests. She wears a black bikini top, and she's loosely arranged her lifeguard shirt so that it protects her bare, strong shoulders. She wears high factors all the time, and her straight freckled nose and full lips are smeared white with zinc. Thanmai's crow-black hair is tied in a topknot. Her long legs are crossed at the knee, and the only part of her that moves is her bare left foot, tapping up and down on the air. Boys and men passing behind her chair look up at her. Some call up but Thanmai doesn't answer. She's intent on the water. Sun bounces off her mirrored shades.

I miss my wife.

The earth's moved. Shadow blankets the sunbathing areas behind the deep-end chair, and the roadside decking. Empty spaces on the concrete are marked by wetness. The bare ground is thick with empty beer cans, bottles, food and food wrappers, plastic bags, hundreds of butts from joints and cigarettes, empty sunscreen bottles. Small groups of people are still sitting around. Music comes from phones. A fat burned woman is sleeping. She wears a dirty white bra and black football shorts pulled up high. The layers of sunburn make her skin glow oddly in the softening afternoon light.

Stranger instructs the people over the PA:

Put your rubbish inna the bin. Put your rubbish inna the bin.

I feel the small hand on my foot again, and call down.

Hey, I told you, you can't dive from this board.

It's me, Thanmai says, it's time to move round.

I swing down from my chair, close my eyes, and step from the poolside down into the water. I sink to the bottom, count to ten, exhale and rise gently to the surface. The water is cold and silky, and I feel a rush all the way through to my insides.

Here's Araba and the kids! Araba's wearing old rugby shorts, sandals and vest. She's hot and tired. Rose, already in her bikini – she must have changed in the car – crashes into my legs.

Hi Dadda! Is Tia still here?

Over there, I say, on the decking at the shallow end.

OK, bye Dadda! and she runs off.

Don't run!

Jay hugs me without smiling or saying anything.

I've missed you, I say. Are you OK?

She's wearing a fleece and blue jeans. Her face is tired and pale. Blue veins stand out around her dark eyes. I lift her face to me.

Are you all right Bear?

I'm fine, she says, and wanders off to the poolside, where she kneels down and pokes at the water with a stick she's carrying.

Araba says: She hardly ate or slept at Dad's. And then the money.

She'll be all right.

I am full of sunshine. I want to drink some cold beer after work. If I say it will be all right maybe Jay won't shout and scream on this, the last Sunday of summer. Even if she does it will pass. I kiss Araba's warm cheek. I'm ready to move on.

Araba doesn't respond to my kiss. She won't be soothed. She's looking over at Jay, pale and clothed in the crowd of suntanned shouting kids. Aren't the holidays nearly over for everyone?

Araba says: If you ask her what the matter is she says she doesn't know.

It'll pass, I say. Something else will happen. You'll see.

Araba lets go of my hand and moves towards her daughter.

Brixton, London, 2005

In late sunlight on Brixton Station Road, Jeff the Chef cooks jerk chicken on the oil-drum grill that stands beside his food wagon. The smoking meat makes my stomach growl. Spiced smoke drifts past men drinking coffee outside Max's railway arch cafe as a commuter train rumbles over their heads. Cigarettes on the table. Phones and prayer beads.

A week of unbroken Indian summer. These warm days are deceptive. Cold and darkness are closer than we think. For now, men whose shops and food wagons are in shade sit in the sun on the other side of the street from their businesses, on holiday from their lives. Some have beers open – bottles of cold Sagres, I'd love one. The hum of many voices speaking many languages. All the different stories. The oceans people have crossed to be here, the people left behind. How good the beer must taste after history.

A man in the sun shouts: This could be the last of it.

Sitting on the pavement outside Herbal Town, shirt open to the waist, his back against a wall (he's Ethiopian, I think, there's a Coptic cross tattooed on his wrist).

You never know, another man, unseen, says.

As we come down the steps from the Recreation Centre, and into the street crowded with men and women talking, I look at Jay. All this is home for her. She's known nothing else.

Why am I living in this place and time? Why this skin and body and not another?

Does Jay notice how the red plastic chairs outside Max's become ruby-coloured in shadow, or wonder what the upright, turbanned Rasta in pressed cords is thinking as he stands guard – or maybe just having a smoke break – outside Ashok's off-licence? Does she think about the people on the trains passing above us, where they are going and what they're dreaming? Does she even hear the trains above all this different music, soaring hymns from Beautiful Books Bible shop, roots and culture rumbling from Bushman's Kitchen?

What about the wildflowers – cowslip, St John's wort, yellow rattle – somehow quivering in light between the brickwork and train tracks above us? How did they get up there?

Often she is an island presence. Far away even when close by, haloed by an isolating light. Some of us are like that more than others, especially when we're kids. I give Jay's silences heavy weight and shade. I take nothing she does for granted. She has her own visions.

I'd guess her head is where we've just come from, the basement gym inside the rec where for the last hour and a half she has played football with and against boys. While she plays I have to bite down on the urge to call out or shout at her. Now there's something Jay's not saying – I can almost hear her talking to herself, to me. Disturbance transmits from her as spiced smoke stings my eyes.

We walk past bright stands of flowers, zinnias and forget-me-nots, red poppies and cornflowers, growing in boxes made from old furniture. Here's a spray of marigolds in an open drawer. The boxes are painted: Malcolm X, a red parrot, tropical vines.

Dirty pigeons eddy at my feet and I kick them away.

Look at the flowers Bear, I say.

She doesn't answer. I'm always saying things like that.

When's the next World Cup Dad? she says.

Next summer. All your countries are in it.

Yay.

I love it here, I say, as we walk through the market at Popes Road and turn left onto Atlantic.

Jay laughs, but she's still inside herself.

I can almost believe in the permanence of these warm days, this unchanging child whose hand fits mine. But I can feel the cold and the darkness coming, and I can't help noticing how the streets and the faces around me are changing all the time. New people with more money are moving in. Once familiar places and people are gone before you miss them, but you do miss them. Soon this will no longer be the place I know.

Jay almost comes up to my shoulder.

When did you get so big?

Jay's heart-shaped face relaxes as we get nearer home, but her skin is dark around her eyes.

Jay won't do anything she doesn't want to, but with me she'll still do things she might not like to get my praise. I'm waiting for her to say I'm not her dad. I'm shy with my authority because the more I become her dad the more terrified I am that she'll say I'm not. Maybe she thinks the same. That if she doesn't do what I want I won't love her.

We don't talk about it. We have great wrestling games that are dances of pure love.

At courtside, Headman's eyes blaze. Jay is scared of him, she flinches when he shouts. Tony is kinder. There's no fat on either man, not a speck. Both have shaved heads. Headman's head is so smooth – like he shaves it twice a day. His fibrous arm and leg muscles gleam under the gym lights.

These men have been finding and training players for over twenty years. If Headman says you're good, scouts from the big London clubs will want to check you out.

Watch this boy in black knee socks, short Afro, shunt the boy in grey Adidas sweats off the ball (at the beginning of the session, Headman won't blow for a foul unless the boys are actually attacking each other. A couple of times Jay had to fight back tears when she got chopped and the foul wasn't given). Afro has the ball, but he won't look up, and he'll never pass, certainly not to Jay. He loses the ball and sits on the floor, rolling his knee socks up and down and moaning loudly to Headman and Tony.

Headman looks disgusted. Tony says, Get up and get on with it, son. For many of the boys, these are the only men who try to teach them discipline and self-respect.

Dionne, the other girl here, has speed and power. She's also bigger than everybody else. She wears a baggy black T-shirt and black shorts. Moving forward, scattering boys, the ball sticks to her feet. Stopping in the middle of the court, head up, she easily holds off the four or five smaller boys who buzz helplessly around her, and then fall back, complaining when she beats them. In play, Dionne's face is set in a hard, dark mask, but whenever Headman shouts praise she smiles a dazzling, melt your heart smile. This hot, subterranean hall contains many hearts in need of love.

Jay's knocked over again. She doesn't complain, doesn't roll around or throw her arms about. She gets up, jogs back over towards the action and then makes a run forward into a tiny space – that's it! Here, here, she says quietly, hands palms out. I want to shout at her: Demand the ball!

She looks over at me. Fearfully, or for help? I wave her forward. Jay begins making arcing runs into the box, her thick plait swinging high. Dionne sits deep and starts looking for her, but either the ball or Jay's run is blocked. At last a ball gets through and Jay's there! She smashes it left-footed, the ball whacks against the foot of the post, then flies away into the crowd of people watching at court-side: mums, aunties, nans, loaded down with food shopping hanging from pushchairs, more kids – really little ones – running around and straying onto the court, their yells amplified under the vaulted ceiling, rushing to collect the ball when it gets kicked out of play. I'm one of the few men here.

Next, Dionne ploughs through a field of panting, disorganized boys, plays a one-two with Jay. Jay's return pass is perfect, soft, and without breaking stride Dionne slams the ball past the keeper, in a Barcelona shirt, so hard the mini-goal is knocked back a foot.

Somebody says, 'Low it man, she's a *baller*.

Headman blasts on his whistle. Tony starts collecting the balls and putting them in the big mesh bags. Jay trudges over to me. Her hair's all wild and frizzed at the front. She's sweaty and panting. I'm careful not to hug or kiss her in front of the boys. I shake her hand and give her a carton of Ribena. She sucks down hard on the straw. She's really thirsty – so am I, my mouth is dry. With a big slurp sound the carton collapses in on itself as Jay empties it and sucks the air out.

Jay puts her hoody on. I put my arm lightly round her shoulders and we walk over to Headman and Tony. Tony is putting everything away. He's finding lost shoes for kids, and talking to the mums. Headman's just standing, his eyes spitting fire. What's he thinking?

Tony: You did good. You enjoy it?

I have my hand on her back and can feel the heat through her hoody.

Jay: It was good.

Headman, his eyes blazing, says: I know it's tough, but you must be tough right back. I know you're good, but are you tough?

Does he think Jay's soft? Does he think I'm soft? I think he only cares about the boys, but then what about Dionne? Maybe it's just me he doesn't take seriously. His look says: why are you bringing her here? Because I want to see how good she really is. Is that what Jay wants? I thought it was. I think that what I'm doing is for the best – if she can play here then getting into a good girls' team will be easy. Fulham are already asking about her. I dream about her playing for Arsenal. She wears 4 and VIEIRA on her shirt. When Jay was little I'd always tell her to watch Vieira. See how he gets up and down the pitch, I tell her.

—

In the street, a young barefoot black woman with close-cropped hair, eyes too big for her face, wrapped in a Portuguese flag, weaves past us holding a can of White Lightning. It's clear from her naked shoulders and the way her body moves underneath the sheer material of the flag that she's wearing nothing else. She's familiar, you'll see her most days, sometimes with other drinkers or users, walking out of time with everybody else. I don't think she has a pimp, though maybe that's him, there, sitting on the wall a few yards away from her, watching her from under a sharp felt hat. Her eyes aren't seeing things the way I'm seeing them. Is everything radiant where she is, softened by a golden wash? Is it worth it? Men coo and talk after her but nobody tries to touch her. Maybe she appears as a vision, maybe they're all used to her.

She is soft-looking, but protected somehow – some force field made of the innocence she projects, even in the state she's in – or by her pimp, if that's who that is, and who I overhear saying to another man: It is not a she, it is a he.

Is that possible?

My arm is still around Jay's shoulders as we cross onto Railton Road, where we live.

Not so good tonight.

The boys don't pass to me Dad.

You have to earn the right to play your own game. You have to go in there and win the ball. When they see how good you are they'll want you on their team.

No they won't Dad.

What are you saying, you don't want to go back?

She's silent the rest of the way home.

That night Araba says: She goes because you want her to.

I wish I'd had somebody pushing me when I was her age.

She's not you.

It'll help her.

She doesn't like it. It scares her.

She needs to toughen up.

Why?

Because she's really good, but she's too self-conscious when she plays with kids she doesn't know.

She's self-conscious because she doesn't want to be there and she's afraid she'll upset you.

From where she's playing on the floor with her Sylvanian animals Rose says: I hate football Dadda.

The little animals – red squirrels, dogs and rabbits – come in family groups of four: mum and dad, boy and girl. You can tell which is which by the clothes they wear (the male hedgehogs wear dungarees, the females have pretty frocks). Rose likes to undress them and jumble them up so that rabbits live with squirrels, dogs with hedgehogs.

After her bath, I watch Jay drawing manga faces in her sketchbook, a tough but paper-sensitive kid, made of hot blood I can see pumping through thick veins under her skin, and wonder, what's she thinking about? About her blood father, now that she knew I wasn't him? I didn't know enough, then, to realize she was always free from my projections and obsessions.

Mostly she's just a kid playing and dreaming. Joyous.

She's busy discovering and assembling the component parts of herself. Keeping some, discarding others. Which part of me is Greek (her blood father was Greek), which part Ghanaian?

She loves and takes for granted what her body can do. Run fast and for ever. Keep a football under close control, use a table-tennis bat – a cricket bat, a tennis racket, anything, pilot a kayak.

She's got kayaking tomorrow. I need to find a pair of neoprene gloves. There's some that will fit her around here someplace.

This was what we worried about in those days. Do the kids have all they need for tomorrow? Where should Jay play football to be the best player she could be? Did that even matter, where will she be happiest? Where should Lee go to university to study Spanish? How many friends can Rose have to stay for a sleepover? And money, we always worried and fought about money in those days.

I think if Jay could have stayed as she was, she would have. I understood too late that what Jay hated was her girlness being noticed   and in the sessions in the rec all the boys were also black, it's true, which is only to say, because no two boys looked alike, that her light skin made her doubly visible. She wanted to disappear into the anonymity of boyhood. She wasn't to know this was a dream. When she outgrew her football boots she didn't want a new pair.

When her body began to change I saw only a greater beauty. I praised her when she got her period, and because she loved me she tried to smile. Was one of the reasons she began to cut herself so she could decide when she would bleed?

'What has happened to me?' Gregor Samsa asks when he wakes up to find himself transformed into a giant insect. 'It was no dream.'

All this is not mine, Jay said, and taped and bound herself, and fought her body with kitchen knives hidden in her room.

Herne Hill, London, 2010

The screaming feels permanent, like hunger, or being lost at sea.

Jay's almost fourteen. It's happened before, whenever she has to go back to school, but never as bad as this. Her face is pale. Her hair, recently cut short for the first time, darker now so that it's almost black, greasy, is wet with sweat at the ends. She's sweating through her pyjamas. The skin around her fingers is ripped and bitten until it bleeds. There are long drifts of white toilet paper on and under Jay's bed. Some of the paper is bloody, and there are cuts on her wrists. Her eyes are too wide and dark, like the kids in the manga comics she loves. I sit at the end of her bed. She's staring at a place far beyond me, beyond this room, sour with blood and sweat, and screaming.

She is not present. I can't reach her. Only Jay's mother can help her. Araba holds her daughter. She won't let go.

What is it Bear?

Jay can't speak. She's carrying a truth she doesn't have the words for. She knows something nobody else in the world does. Maybe she can't believe the words she'll have to say.

Bear Bear, hey, come on, what is it?

How can she make us believe her? Believe what she is?

But Araba won't let go, not until Jay tells and somewhere, wherever she is, Jay knows this. Jay can't say anything that will stop her mother loving her. Araba will sit holding her all night if she has to, while Jay screams like someone dying or being born.

What's the matter with Jay Dadda?

Rose's lion-coloured hair is frizzed out. She smells of cocoa butter. Together we've done her homework.

I don't know sweetie.

What's this doing to Rose? She's becoming quieter and quieter.

She's sad.

Yes she is. Do you know why?

No Dadda, she says so quietly I can hardly hear.

Suddenly the screaming stops for long enough for me to believe that it's stopped for good. That Jay is herself again. That we might continue with our lives as they were before.

Rose and I look at each other. There are things we can never say to each other. We have to believe in love. Then Jay is crying. Crying but not screaming.

It's late when Araba comes out of Jay's room. What could make Jay so unhappy? For a long time Araba and I had believed that Jay was gay, and that in time she would tell us so. Was this what Jay had been screaming about? Was she being bullied? When Jay was eleven and Rose ten, we moved away from the cooperative housing block where they had lived all their lives. Jay and Rose were losing all their best friends, all at once. Araba and I loved the house on a hill that we moved into, but there were no kids around for Jay and Rose to play with. They had spent all their time in one or other of their friends' houses, or outdoors, but now they began spending a lot of time alone in their rooms.

Araba takes a sip of my wine.

She's not gay, Araba says, she's not being bullied. She won't wear the skirt because she says she's a boy. No, *he's* a boy. We're to call Jay *him*.

I look at Araba.

I know, but Jay says there are other people like him.

Together we go into Jay's room. I think we held hands. She – he – is sitting up, his eyes red raw, his bandaged arms on the bedspread, I recognize Jay again. Like he went out of his body and came back. He seems so sad to be back. Jay looks at me, and I realize he's frightened, like I'm going to tell him off. I hug him.

It's OK Jay, I say, it's OK. And though I understand nothing of what has happened, I say:

It'll be all right Bear. I'm sorry you feel so bad, but it'll be all right.

Jay, crying, lifts his hands and points at the length of his body under the covers.

I just hate all this, he says. I don't want it.

Oh Jay, Araba says.

We have to find out about this, Araba said, opening her laptop. Jay showed me some sites about kids like him.

Have you heard of this before? Araba asked me. Transgender? Jay says he was born in the wrong body. He's a boy who was born a girl.

What do we do?

Jay told me. There's stuff he needs. Something called a binder. And medicine. Look, we have to take him here.

Should we have realized before?

It doesn't matter now.

Swiss Cottage, London, 2012

The blockers will allow space for ongoing therapeutic exploration, the therapist had said.

What does that even mean? Jay said as we walked in the rain back to Swiss Cottage tube station.

It means they think you could change your mind. Not like surgery. You could stop taking the blockers. It's not irreversible.

Like that's ever going to happen, Jay said.

He's sixteen. Tall as me now. Dressed all in black. I'm still having to get to know this boy full of demands and sorrow. Black Harrington jacket, black, low-hung jeans. I've got girly hips and a big arse, he says, tight jeans give me away. Black DM shoes, black beanie.

I don't want to be a boy, Jay had corrected the therapist, I am a boy.

Mate, I said, nothing's going to happen as quick as you want it to, but this is a start.

Maybe, he said.

Not maybe, it's happening.

In the last two years he's learned not to believe in authority or authority's promises. His teachers said they would try and make things easier for him, and then made him use the disabled toilet. Jay stopped going and in the end we took him out of school.

131

OK? I said.

OK Dad.

The hypothalamic blockers will stop Jay's periods by stopping the production of oestrogen by the ovaries, the therapist said, but we don't know how Jay will be affected mentally.

Jay says it's true he's paranoid. He's sure everybody is looking at him, that each person he encounters in a city of millions sees through his attempts to pass a boy.

I still get mis-pronouned all the time, he says. I hate it.

Sometimes when he was small he'd be called as a boy, long hair and all, and he'd smile, secret, shy.

Just believing that somebody is thinking he's a girl can drag him into a deep panic. He cannot allow himself to verbalize his anger when, for example, he is mis-pronouned or when people he knows and has thought of as friends are cruel to him, because when he is angry his voice – that he is training himself to deepen, smoking for the same reason, though he smokes mostly for stress and because he thinks it makes him look cool – goes high, and he believes he will be found out for what he is: a teenage boy trapped in a teenage girl's body.

What do you do when it happens? the therapist asked. When somebody calls you a girl. Jay shrugs.

He stays in bed, in the dark, sometimes for days. He wanders through the house at night when everybody else is asleep. He smokes in the garden. He cuts himself with the knives he hides in his room. He can believe in no future.

The surgery he needs to become whole seems so far in the distance as to not exist in any reality he can imagine for himself. He cuts his body again and again in his anger and frustration. Finally he goes out and stays out and doesn't come home. He gets drunk. Won't answer his phone. When it's worse than this he talks about killing himself, and his mother and I are scared to leave the house. I remember going into his room once – his bed a messed heap of stale and dirty bedclothes red with blood. Piles of bloody tissues on the floor and in the bed. Jay's arm bloody red and gaping with long cuts. His lovely face pale and blank with sorrow.

Jay looks at his hands. Does he see the ripped skin around his fingers?

But sometimes it's OK to be outside?

Yeah.

What do you do then?

I sit in coffee shops mostly.

What is it about coffee shops?

We're really listening, me and Araba. We want to know. He hardly says anything at home. Do you talk about how you're feeling? the therapist asks him. I don't want to upset Mum and Dad, Jay says.

I can sit there and nobody bothers me, Jay says.

What do you do in the coffee shop?

I write, Jay says. I write mostly.

Araba says: How long does he have to be on the blockers before he can begin testosterone treatment?

Jay dreams about the ways testosterone will turn him into himself.

The therapist looks through his weaved fingers to the floor.

If we decide to put Jay on the blockers it will be for a year. And then we'll decide about testosterone.

Jay looks like he's been punched hard and is trying to show it doesn't hurt.

Araba puts her hand on my closed fist. She looks at me. There's no air in this room.

I don't like the way this therapist (distracted? professionally neutral?) talks to us. I don't like his pauses after Araba has asked him a question. When my wife talks, or when I talk, he looks as if he's trying to hear something beyond the noise we're making. He has decided what he thinks about us by what we look like.

A large, awkward, heavily tattooed white man, holding on to his anger. A frayed black woman, leaning forward in her seat, radiating love. Close to desperation.

I'm sure he thinks we're stupid. Maybe that's just my desperation (and it's about class, too, I know). Come on, I think, do your job. Help my son! I want to say: I know these binary oppositions are useless! I know that Jung asked: what have we done with our twin sister who we abandoned at birth?

The boy Jay's becoming includes the girl he was. But he is a boy. He doesn't need to suffer any more until you're satisfied he won't change his mind. What I'm scared of is what he's going to do while he's waiting for his life to start.

For somebody else to tell him he can start living? You're only going to be sixteen once, I tell him. As distressing as this is, you're free to be who you want. Jay's look tells me I have no idea what he's going through.

He's waited too long, I say suddenly.

We come here and we talk but something needs to happen. When we came here for the first time we thought he'd be put on testosterone straight away. Maybe that was our fault, we didn't understand how long everything takes. How many kids you see like Jay. But it's too hard for him now. We can't stand to see him suffering. Do you have any idea how difficult it is for him just to walk out of the door?

The therapist doesn't say anything. And I like him, suddenly, for not claiming to know how Jay feels.

I can feel Jay looking at me. Without realizing it I am crying.

When he leaves here he needs dates in his diary, Araba says. So he knows that this starts then, and then this happens, do you understand?

Walking to the tube Araba's phone rings. She walks away to answer it.

You all right? I say to Jay.

He's looking at me. *Dad was crying.* Dad's soft, he told the therapist once, soft meaning something good.

That was Rose, Araba said. She wants to know why there's never anybody *fucking* home when she gets in from school. Then she hung up on me. I need to call her back.

You guys get back, Jay said.

What are you going to do?

I'm going to hang out for a bit. Maybe go and see Dusty.

You going to be all right?

Yes.

Sure?

Yes Dad.

All right. Answer your phone. Have you got your keys?

Yes Dad.

All right. See you later. I love you.

Love you too Dad. Love you Mum.

Stockwell, London, 2012

The young doctor – open-faced, matter-of-fact but serious, aware what this means to Jay without making a fuss about it – we like him immediately – holds a syringe of powder and another of clear liquid. He's reading the instructions that came with the package of syringes and needles the nurse brought to his office.

Stockwell Group Practice. The noise from the packed waiting room does not reach us here. This room is small and too hot. The fabric covering my seat is scratchy. The air is dry and gritty. You don't often hear good news in these places, but Jay's finally beginning the course of hormone blockers. He'll take these for a year and then begin testosterone treatment. Then it will be another year before he can have top surgery. Today though, Jay is happy. The doctor reads the instructions, looks at the syringes he's holding then back at the instructions.

Jay is sitting on the edge of his chair. His attention is riveted on the syringes.

My hand is on the back of Jay's dirty neck – dirty because he's a teenager, or because he's trans?

The mixture only stays stable for a short while, the doctor says. That's why it's not made ahead of time. I like the way he talks to Jay. He starts to introduce the liquid into the powder.

I've never done this before, he says.

We all laugh nervously.

Jay's already rolled his sleeve up. I can feel the excitement almost bursting from him. Something's finally happening! The doctor says nothing about the dozens of scars. He pushes the needle in. Jay hates needles but he's smiling. When he's finished, he wipes Jay's arm with a disinfectant pad and puts a little plaster over the needle mark.

OK, he says, see you next month.

Jay reaches over and shakes his hand.

Thanks, he says.

All right mate? I say as we come out into cold air on Stockwell Road. The skatepark's already full of kids flinging themselves around. Jay's beaming.

What?

My life started today, he says.

Herne Hill, London, 2012

When the man came home that night the boy was gone. The boy was sixteen and it was to be expected and even hoped for that he would spend so much time out in the city, but since he'd started the new hormone treatment his instability was more frightening to the man than anything that had gone before.

The man mapped the boy's day by the things he'd left behind. He picked up dirty clothes – the boy's T-shirts, his padded boxers and stiff chest binders and put them in the laundry basket. He cleaned the unwashed cereal bowls and teacups with cigarette ends in. The man looked for but did not find the knives he knew the boy hid in his stale and dirty room.

I put down my pen and close my notebook, push back my chair and stand up. I take out the bottle of Heineken I put in the freezer a few minutes ago, open the bottle and take a drink of ice-cold beer. I sigh without meaning to. I go downstairs and out into the garden.

It's a hot night, busy with sirens and loud music. Boys on unsilenced mopeds race through the streets in laps of rising noise. The honeysuckle on the garden wall is ragged and needs looking after though the scent is wonderful. Jay is smoking. He tries to hide the cigarette when I come outside.

Go ahead and smoke, I say. It's all right. I mean, it's not all right but it's all right.

Jay is hunched over. His thick black hair is cut short and damp with sweat. He is wearing black jeans and a black T-shirt that once belonged to me, and he's barefoot. His pale arms are a mess of cuts and scars. The newest cuts are deepest and longest. If I tell him to wash up, or not smoke in his room, or flush the toilet when you've had a shit, for God's sake, will he run away? Will he harm himself?

He puts out his cigarette and lights another.

You OK? I say. I feel like I haven't seen you for weeks. You're not up when I go to work and I'm asleep when you come back from wherever you go every night.

Jay smokes and makes a small, distressed noise.

I reach over and take the lighter from Jay's hand. I light my roll-up and put the lighter back in the his lap. I stroke his head.

The valley of Wied Il Ghasri in Gozo begins at Ta Dbiegi Hill, passes down through the village of I-Ghasri and on between iz Zebbug and Ta' Gurdan Hill, before ending in a narrow channel of sea wedged tight between steeply rising limestone cliffs.

The man and his wife and their thirteen-year-old daughter, who they had called Kate but who, in the last month or so, had stopped answering to that name, had once looked down into the deep ravine at the clear water shining like a needle far below.

They stood by the first of a long sequence of rough steps that led down to the beach.

"Wow Daddy," Kate said.

The man who had told them about the dive had said there were one hundred steps.

"After you get down to the beach," he'd told them, "you'll

need to surface-swim about three hundred yards before dropping down at the point where the water becomes open sea. Keep to the wall on your right-hand side. You can't miss the entrance to the cave. It's a tough entry," the diver had said when Kate asked him, "but it's worth it."

The man did not know whether he would be able to make it down the winding steps to the beach where they would enter the water and begin the dive. It was not the number of steps, or that he would have to carry the heavy kit, but the old conviction that he would fall. There was nothing to stop him but a single wooden rail that he would not trust with the weight of all that he would be carrying. Dark, crescent-winged swifts wheeled and swooped against the pale cliffs below. In the bar he had been excited to hear about the cave. Now, he knew that if he had not had Kate with him he would not have tried.

"Why's the water green so close to the beach Daddy," she said, "when the rest of it's blue?"

She was lying flat on her stomach with her head and shoulders stuck out over the edge of the cliff. He looked at her – rangy and long-limbed in her vest and shorts. Her close-cropped black hair was wet with sweat at the roots. He had to tell himself not to call her back from the edge.

"I think it's the vegetation under the surface that makes it look green," he said, "the water there is pretty shallow. What do you think," he said to his wife, who was standing close to the car with her arms folded, a red-chequered headscarf over her long dark hair.

"I'm not going."

"Why not?"

"I'm just not."

"I'll carry your kit down."

"No."

She got back into the rental car that had the three wetsuits draped over it to try and dry them out between dives. She closed the door, and the man watched her reach to turn on the air conditioning.

He had got lost trying to find the place, and they had driven for a long time on single-track unpaved roads that had all looked the same. Driving over the broken, signless tracks they were thrown around inside the car. Kate laughed. His wife's lips were drawn back tight against her teeth and she did not speak.

Is it just everything Jay, I say, or something new I need to know about?

It's just, it's really hot Dad, you know? I can't breathe.

You want to take your binder off? I mean, you're home. You're safe here.

Jay shakes his head.

You haven't been happy in a while, I say. Why is that, do you think?

Jay shrugs and plays with his cigarette pack. The pack is covered in writing and little drawings.

I don't mean happy. You know what I mean. I know it must be harder in the summer. I mean, I know it must be harder to pass, and you must be uncomfortable all the time.

Jay smokes, holding the cigarette in his left hand and rubbing his eyes with the heel of his right.

Not uncomfortable, that's a useless word, I say, and bend to crush my roll-up in the ashtray by Jay's foot. I stand up and exhale hard. I drink some beer and put the bottle on the ground.

I'm trying to write about all this, I say. I think it can help us both to write about it.

OK.

Is it OK though? Really?

Jay looks up at me.

Yeah Dad, he says. Go for it.

The man drank from a bottle of water and he poured water over his head and over Kate's head. She carried her black fins and wore a khaki belt with a two-kilo lead weight on each hip.

"See you down there, Dad," she said.

He watched her walking down the steps, flat-chested in the compressive wetsuit, her short black hair tamped down and shining with water. The yellow dust his daughter raised from the rough steps stuck to her damp neoprene dive boots. He watched her until she passed beneath a limestone overhang and disappeared.

"Have you had a pee?" he called after her.

"Dad!"

"Try not to pee in your wetsuit," he called again, "we have to take it back to the dive shop, remember, and it's really hard to get rid of the smell."

"Dad!!"

He opened the boot of the big car to get the kit.

"Aren't you at least going to go with her down to the beach?" he said to the back of his wife's head.

"What for?" she said. She hadn't turned to look at him, but he'd been able to tell she'd been crying.

"Why would you even ask me that," he said. "For niceness. To see she doesn't fall."

"She doesn't want me anywhere near her."

That morning his wife had found Kate in the bathroom, her chest carefully wrapped in toilet paper, stuffing a small rolled wad of paper down inside her shorts.

Sweating freely, he lifted the two sets of heavy kit and stood them carefully next to a big rock.

"Christ," he said, before slamming the boot closed.

I can't imagine what it's like for you, I say. All I can tell you is that you will get to where you want to be.

You can't promise me that, Jay says. He makes a hiccupping sound and rubs his eyes again.

No, I can't, because who knows what will happen. In the meantime I don't think it helps to think about your life the way you do.

What way?

Like there's a before and after. Like everything's going to be all right after you start T, or when you have surgery. Remember you thought that about the blockers. Like everything would be all right.

I know.

Do you? You're still cutting yourself.

The heat and the weight of the tank and the steel backplate dug into his neck and shoulders as he walked carefully down over the sun-bleached dusty steps. The voices of sunbathers on the little beach were loud in the ravine. Wild thyme and purple heather grew on the cliff side. Yellow crown daisies grew on the shore. Kate waited for him by the bright water.

They swam on their backs through the inlet towards the open sea. A matching narrow ribbon of blue sky showed between the tops of the yellow cliffs. A sunburnt man called after them from the beach.

"There's nothing down there," he said.

Kate, wearing her mask and black hood, kept flipping over to look under the water.

"Sea grass," she said happily, in a voice made deep by the mask she was wearing. "Sea grass and big yellow boulders and little silver fish."

They swam in bright water, through clouds of fiery cardinals and silver damselfish, until he saw the indistinct dark break in the reef wall. Using his torch to light their way, they swam over dark boulders until they were inside the huge domed interior of the cave.

He swam ahead, into the heart of the cave, and then turned to look back at what he had come to see. The dark entrance they had swum through was now the opening to the sun-lightened blue sea, radiant and shimmering in the darkness, and in the centre of it was Kate, coming to him out of the light.

They ascended together, and once at the surface, and inside the cave, the blue light at the entrance was below and shining up at them, and the high interior of the cave was dark, so dark that the man could not see how far back it went.

"How about that light?" he said.

"Listen Dad," Kate said. "Boom!"

Her voice went out into the darkness of the cave and came back deepened and transformed.

Surf pounded against the roof of the cave.

"What is that Dad?"

"It's just the sea hitting against the outside."

"It's really noisy."

"It sounds like a storm but it's nothing really," he said. "Imagine how scary it would be if it was even a little bit rough."

"I'm not a bit scared," Kate said. "I like it here. I feel safe."

"Why?"

"Oh, I don't know. I just like it. Ask me my name Dad."

"What's your name?"

"Joe!" she shouted, against the noise of the crashing world outside. "My name is Joe! JOE!"

"You ready to go back Joe?" he said.

"I guess so."

"You want to lead?"

"Yes!"

"You know where you're headed? Just swim towards the light. That's the opening."

"Obviously."

"OK, but which way do you go when you're through the other side?"

"Keep the wall to your left," she said, spitting in her mask and rinsing it before putting it back on.

"Then just follow it home."

It just feels like nothing's happening Dad, Jay says. Like this is going to be for ever. I'm such a freak.

You're not a freak, we've talked about that. That's not going to help you.

I put my arms around my son.

You are my brave, strong boy, I say, and kiss Jay's dirty head. You just have to hold on.

Herne Hill, London, 2013

Dusty is dyeing Jay's hair.

They've been up there for hours. There's lots of laughing and splashing. I'm determined not to ask them to turn the music down. I know I'll have to clean the bathroom when they've finished but I don't mind. They better not flood the place!

Dusty is ethereal but nobody's fool. It's hard to say what the natural colour of her short-cropped hair is, because she dyes it all the time (today it's pink) but her skin is almost transparently white.

Jay and Dusty have known each other for ever but now they're boyfriend and girlfriend. Jay says Dusty's mum doesn't like him going round there. Some people can't make room in their heads for Jay, for who he is, and for what they see when they see him and Dusty together. How's Jay supposed to understand why people hate him for existing?

The kids fight of course. Dusty's sweetness is not the whole story.

I'm sick of you! Dusty shouted at him once. I'm going to get a real boy!

Gender is performative Daddy, Rose told me earlier. Dusty has helped Rose dye her hair too, and I can hear my daughter's music over the racket of her hairdryer and blasts of singing.

—

I've given up trying to work in this din. I'm just looking at the flowers in two vases on the kitchen table, creamy freesias and daffodils, and the clay bowl full of bright orange mandarins.

There's a big party in Camberwell tonight. Dusty and Jay and Rose and all their friends are going. Some people at the party will know Jay is trans, and others won't. Will the people he know keep his secret? Will somebody get drunk and tell? What will he do then? He hasn't been to a party in a long time.

Jay and Dusty come down the stairs giggling, music playing from a phone. Jay's so pale you wouldn't believe he's mixed-race. His hair's wrapped in a towel. He's wearing a grubby binder and no T-shirt, boxers, and odd socks. I almost don't notice his scars.

Look at your great big hairy legs, I say.

He beams at me. Shuffles past pretending to be an old man and making old man noises.

Dusty wears a white T-shirt and short cut-offs. Hair wrapped in a towel, too. She's even paler than Jay. She's carrying bottles of hair dye.

Hello Dusty, how are you love? How's art school?

I'm good, she says in her soft voice, how are you?

I hug her. I want to thank her for Jay's happiness today.

Light streams in through the floor-to-ceiling windows.

The kids make tea and toast and ignore me. I look at Jay. Boys his age most often have a visible Adam's apple, stubble. Jay's face is smooth, and he's pretty. He smokes, practises lowering his voice. What frustrates him the most is being seen as a *dyke*. Nothing against dykes, but he's a straight boy.

Testosterone will bulk him up, deepen his voice, make hair grow on his face. This is why he's so desperate to be put on it, but he's got another month or so to wait, he has to be eighteen. For now, he's on the blockers, which means he lives with really low energy levels and major mood swings.

At the Tavistock Centre, where we go for therapy with Jay, where the therapist I didn't like has been replaced by a woman we all love, and where the support group, Gendered Intelligence, have their monthly meetings, I watch the trans boys. There's a definite look: short hair, often shaved close at the back and sides, hats – trucker caps or beanies – low-slung baggy jeans, trainers, often Vans or Converse. A lot of looking down, faces set to blank, whether out of fear and unhappiness, or an approximation of the hard mask boys often wear. I watch the dads, too (all of us trying hard to look like there's nothing unusual about being here), recalibrating our speech and body language to masculine when we talk to our new sons. I call Jay 'mate' all the time, I'm always ruffling his hair and play punching him. What do the dads who don't come think? The ones who think there's something wrong with their child?

I took Jay to an old-fashioned barber's the first time he had his hair cut really short. You've got a good head of hair mate, the barber told him. Didn't get it from your dad, eh? Jay loved all the piss-taking, he couldn't stop smiling.

Rose is right, gender is performative. Outside this house, Jay is constantly enacting a performance of boyhood to pass as a boy (while, unknown to Jay though I've tried to explain it to him, the boys are doing the same thing).

The boys on the corner who race mopeds in the street and act tough for each other would have noticed that a girl had moved into the house, a tomboy for sure but a girl, definitely (a beautiful girl). And a couple of years later the girl was gone and a boy was coming out of the house. A tall, awkward-looking boy, looking at the ground except when he remembered to look up, with short dark hair and glasses and dressed in black and smoking, always smoking. I don't think they've said anything to him, but I wouldn't know. I don't want to think these boys are a threat to my son, but I have to consider it.

When the kids have got what they need the dog follows them downstairs.

In the bathroom I pick up wet towels, and clean the dye out of the bath. I'm happy doing these normal dad things. It's not blood I'm washing away.

It gets dark. There's lots of toing and froing downstairs. Voices are raised, occasional shrieks of laughter. Jay's bedroom door opening and closing and feet padding along the hallway to the toilet. Somebody turns the tumble dryer on. The dog comes back upstairs.

Did you get any toast? I say to her.

All this time I can hear Rose singing.

Finally they're ready.

Rose! Jay shouts.

I'm coming! Rose shouts from her room. Don't shout at me!

Let's have a look at you, I say.

I go downstairs to where they are standing in the hall, smiling. Dusty wears a silver minidress, silver shoes with little buckles, and white tights. Her hair is silver.

Jay's hair is jet-black, black as the night sky, and swept back in a big quiff. He's dressed all in black. Black leather jacket and black boots.

Rose comes down the stairs singing and carrying a battered pair of steel-toecapped DMs. She's wearing an old Levi's black cord jacket that used to belong to me (decorated with her badges: The Clash, Trojan Records, Haile Selassie) over a long black dress she's borrowed from her mother. Ghanaian Gye Nyame earrings, red lipstick, dyed black hair in thick plaits.

The kids are beaming at each other and play-fighting their way out of the door. I am happy to be jealous. Of their youth and beauty. Freedom. Everything in front of them.

Wow, I say, fantastic. You look like the future.

Unknown

I don't know how long Jason had been dead before I found
out, or who told me. I can't remember where I was – I
couldn't have been where I think – or be certain of the date.

When I heard that he was dead I saw myself pissing on
Jason's grave, darkening the freshly dug ground and wet-
ting the granite headstone. The phone's heat, the voice and
pictures in my head, made my face warm.

I was in my thirties, a father myself, a long-distance
swimmer and diver. I was beloved.

It must have been 1997. The reason I sometimes doubt
this is because I'm almost certain Robin told me, but I left
her in 1995. I also remember Robin calling me at the theatre
bookshop, where Araba and I first met, to tell me, but I
had left there in '96, so that's not possible, though it's what
I remember.

Jason died just before or just after Rose, his blood granddaughter, was born. I was living on my own in Maze Hill,
close to the river. There was a brewery nearby, and my flat
was saturated with the bittersweet smells of hops and
barley. I'd stay with Araba, Lee and Jay for days at a time in
the house she was renting in Nunhead. I decorated a room
for Jay and the new baby, but I always had the flat to go
back to. There were doubts on both sides. Sometimes
Araba would send me away. Sometimes I'd have to go.

Steve drove me to Araba's when she went into labour. She'd called him to get me. I didn't have a phone. It was the middle of the night, I remember, and Steve had to bang on my door for a long time before I woke up.

Another homebirth, but not quick like Jay. I follow Araba from room to room in the muted light trying to find a good place where she can settle, but she is beyond my reach. When Rose is here at last there is heavy bruising on her face from the pressure. She can hardly open her eyes, which are bloodshot. Araba is bleeding too much. Her face flutters and I think she's going to faint but she comes back and the bleeding stops. Rose yells suddenly and we laugh.

Somehow in the warm May morning we are all together in the garden. My heart's still beating fast as I hold my daughter. When I call, Mum is overjoyed about her new granddaughter.

Did Mum tell me Jason was dead? I don't remember. Mum always loved Robin, for a long time she hoped we'd get back together, so it makes sense that she would have asked her. It tells you about Robin that she agreed to call me.

Robin's mum – Sylvia – was killed around this time, in a terrible car crash. Was it this Robin rang to tell me about, and not Jason – how the car her mother was driving was smashed into, and how she was hit again and killed as she waited by the side of the road for the ambulance? Robin's loss was greater than mine.

It was only after Jason died that I began looking for news of him online. There wasn't much. My father's name appears on a few sites listing business data. The credit ratings of companies and company directors. On his page is a long list of dissolved companies. I might have bought the reports (I still could). Find out about outstanding court judgements and unpaid mortgages. Key areas of risk. I tell myself it isn't language I understand.

In a court bankruptcy notice published in 1984, Jason is listed as: of no present occupation, lately residing at White Roofs, Bramble Lane, Wrecclesham, Farnham, Surrey, previously at High Down Cottage, Red Bird Road, Headley Down, Hampshire, and formerly carrying on business as a travel consultant and retailer of leisure products under the name of Commercial and Leisure Facilities from 77 Great Windmill Street, London W.1.

No present occupation. Lately residing. Previously. Formerly. Nothing solid there. Long gone from all those places. The record shows fourteen dissolved companies but these are only the most recent. A man who knew told me how it works. The long con or long game. Form a company, place an order for goods, pay for goods, get credit from the suppliers as a good credit risk, use credit on a huge order of transportable goods you don't pay for, sell goods for cash at knockdown prices, disappear leaving a huge debt.

Why didn't I find out more? I couldn't ask Mum, it's true, but it wouldn't have taken much to find him when he was alive. Did I like how not having a dad made me feel? It gave me an excuse for the weakness inside me that made me feel like a wall that had not been coursed, so that I was loose mud, ready to give way at any time. Why was I like this if it wasn't because of him? These things were not my responsibility so there was nothing I could do about them.

He hadn't wanted to know about me, had he?

One Sunday evening in September, when Jay was twelve, and just beginning to be really unhappy (we had bought a dog, a black Lab, specially for her) I opened an email that said, I think I must be your sister. Corrina. She'd read something I'd written.

It was her. My brother was the only other person I'd seen with hair that shade of red. She was Luke's twin all right. She had these big wide eyes, golden almost, and her red hair was long.

I jumped straight in. Told her she was beautiful. Sent a picture of Luke and me, drunk on my fortieth. I'd always wanted a sister, I said. Did she want to meet up? We agreed to meet the following Sunday. She liked the picture of me and Luke. Well, I thought, at least she can see what we're like.

I took the black puppy. Corrina's big eyes got bigger when she saw me.

I can't believe it, she said, you look just like him.

She petted the puppy.

Oh my God you really do.

Jason loved animals, she said (she was careful at first not to say *Dad*). He couldn't stand to see any living creature hurt.

Luke arrived. I'd phoned him straight away. I was excited to know something he didn't. My brother is compact and powerful. Big outsized hands. Head shaved like mine. High, brick-red cheeks and shining eyes that give nothing away. This was before he went to live in the Gambia. He took to Corrina. Why not, she was our sister! Somebody I had dreamed about all my life was suddenly real, talking and smoking – we were all talking and smoking like mad – her hair dazzling in the autumn sunshine.

What did she see? Did she lay awake at night when she was a little girl and dream about us (Jason had told her when she was little)? We were tough-looking men. We'd run headlong at the world in our different ways and it showed. We were both marked and scarred.

Look, Corrina said, do you want to go for a drink?

We walked over Blackfriars Bridge, to a pub by the river that was full of tourists. We sat outside. It was getting cold but there were heaters and we all wanted to smoke. The dog sat in my lap. When she was bored she got down and mooched about under the table, chewing our cigarette butts, getting her lead tangled up.

When Mum got pregnant, Corrina said, Dad wanted her to have an abortion because he couldn't stand the idea of having to leave me.

Did Luke and I look at one another then, as if to say, did she just say that?

Corrina said: Dad would pick me up from school and drive to the pub. I'd sit doing my homework while Dad drank with his pals.

He wanted me with him when he was dying, she said. It was cancer. Too much smoking and drinking. I'd lay on the bed and hold him and he'd stroke my hair.

Corrina said: I have a brother. Andre was in a state, she

said. He's thirty-two and he's going to end up like Dad. We go for months not talking. He's going to die soon unless he stops.

Would Luke and I meet our brother? Maybe talk to him?

We agreed that we'd meet soon. By this time all three of us were pissed. We put Corrina in taxi.

That's my sister, I told the cabbie.

She was all red hair and long legs getting into the car. Part of me really fancied her.

Take care of her. We just met for the first time.

Right, the cabbie said, that's great!

Luke left and I decided to walk home. It was a long way. The puppy started slowing up and then stopping. Then she stopped altogether and looked up at me with wide eyes. I knew I was making her suffer. I picked her up and carried her.

Andre did not look like his sister or like me or like Luke.

He was small and dark.

He looks like a pikey, Luke said.

We met in my local pub, in Brixton. I was driving all this, me and Corrina. We were the big talkers.

Corrina kept looking from Andre to me and Luke. She was brave. I liked Corrina. She looked like us, and she was warm and funny. I could feel that Luke liked her too.

I wish I could remember what Andre looked like, and what we said to each other. It was a drinking match more than anything. Did Andre feel on the spot? Had he wanted to meet us at all? Is that why he got messed up beforehand (and he was messed up, it was obvious), or was he always like this?

Corrina must have loved Andre very much to risk getting in touch. She had her own reasons for looking for us, I'm sure. She wanted to know about her big brothers, but mostly I think it was about Andre. Corrina wanted her big brothers to take care of him. We'd had to look after ourselves. We were tough. We'd be able to help Andre. She wanted to make everything all right, and I believed in her. She didn't know how we'd react. The story of mine she'd read was about a boy who was lost without his father, and who dreams about brothers and sisters he doesn't know.

All Jason's children together for the first time. It was such a sad table. I remember thinking: There isn't enough drink in the world for the four of us. We are just going to sit here and keep pouring it down for ever. Did Corrina think: All his sons are the same way?

Andre said: I remember Dad coming home and grabbing the vodka bottle and drinking about half of it down straight. 'I needed that,' he said.

Dad never did that, Corrina said.

Yes he did, Andre said, and gulped some of his drink.

Was his skin pale? Were his eyes dark? Certainly I remember his eyes were dark and pinholed. This is what happened to the son who did have Jason for a father. Who wanted to be like him. Andre was a director of a number of dissolved companies, too.

I knew I wouldn't do anything to help him. I can feel Andre's suffering now, why not then? Was it just that I was so angry? Mate, I wanted to say, you've had everything me and Luke didn't have, and look at the state of you.

I can't speak for Luke. But maybe because Jason would have wanted me to, I knew I wouldn't help him. I'd started all this – me and Corrina, and now I was saying fuck it, I don't want this.

What I said to Luke was: I can't have him coming to the house, mate. I won't let him near my kids.

Fuck it, Luke said, I told him I'd lock him in a room and sit with him for as long as it takes, but that's not what he wants. He wants to carry on.

Was Luke thinking what I was? How lucky we were that Jason left us. How lucky we were to have Mum.

I don't remember how the night ended. What was said and what promises, if any, were made. I really can't remember what Andre looked like. An impression of darkness. I can't remember getting home. Was Corrina sad? Did she know as she was leaving with Andre that we'd never see her again?

Are you all right Dadda? Rose said. She was all clean in her pyjamas, bright black nail polish on her little toes.

I picked her up. I held her close and buried my face in her hair. She hugged me tight. Dadda, she said. My dadda.

I held Rose for a beat too long.

I'm sorry I abandoned you, Corrina.

You're getting too big, I said.

Are you pissed? Araba said, her eyes shining as she looked at me.

Yeah, a little bit. Sorry.

It's all right. Put Rose down. We saved you some food. Tell me what happened.

Put me down Dadda.

Ovingdean, East Sussex, 2013

From the train station at Brighton, I walk down Queen's Road and catch a bus to Ovingdean. At St Dunstan's, I walk up onto the downs. It is a bright and cloudless November morning but the ground is soaked.

The sky is a blue wash. The green downland, silver sea and southern sky fold into one another in curves of limitless colour. From up here, I can see the sky reflected in the many windows of St Dunstan's, and in the glass bow that stands in front of the central tower. The clear light burnishes and softens to peach the building's expanse of sandy brick. I wonder about the blind veterans who live there, with all that light and open space they can't see.

I walk from the high downs to a lane that is almost hidden by wild hedgerows. There is a continuous, soft, split-splat sound of water dripping on fallen leaves – brown, olive, bright pale yellow – that lie thick on the path. There are layers of rotted-down leaves below those newly fallen. Soaked prayer flags in the hedgerow – their colours muted – mark where Johann lives. Birds' nests are visible in the palisade of trees around his place.

I open the gate. Dogs bark. I can smell woodsmoke and damp burning leaves. I close the gate and more rainwater falls from the hedgerow. The barking gets louder.

A grey squirrel races along the wet bough of a tree, stripping the branch of the last of its leaves, and making them fall in slow succession. The leaves, yellow and orange fans, slow time as they fall.

Johann puts down the carpenter's plane he's holding and comes stooping through the doorless entrance of his rose-covered cottage. Johann and Kit were together twenty-five years. Now they are separated. Their three children are grown.

Johann's hair is grey, and cropped short. Mantras and charms are tattooed on his hands and fingers. His pale feet are tattooed with swastikas. The old black sandals he's wearing once carried him over the Himalayas. There's sawdust on his blue smock.

Behind him the unhinged door is lying on the sundeck. There's an open toolbox next to the door, and wood shavings on the deck. Dogs come from the house with Johann and bark at me. A small terrier with an underbite that makes him look bad-tempered, and a slow grey mongrel with caramel-coloured nubs for teeth. I bend down to scratch their ears. I can smell the earthy, old dog smell. They stop barking.

Big storms last couple of days, Johann says. Rough weather. Big swells.

It's still now.

Storm's passed. Don't think it will at the time.

That's right. The storm took the door off?

That was me.

The dogs bark again. A postman comes through the gate and up the path carrying a big, heavy-looking satchel. He wears shorts and boots and a fleece. The dogs push themselves against him, their old tails wagging. The postie has a long grey pony tail. His face is weathered but clear. There's a piece of coloured ribbon tied around his left wrist. He bends down and coos to the dogs, scratching behind their ears.

Plenty of fight left, he says.

You going on all right? the postie says to Johann.

I'm going good, Johann says. You?

I'm good, says the postie, digging into his bag and bringing out a pile of packages. He looks up at the winter sun.

Good but slow. Here, he says, these are all yours.

Give us a hand, Johann says to me.

I never get any post, I say.

Send off for stuff, Johann says, his dark eyes shining.

The postie laughs.

We carry the packages into the cottage and put them down. The dogs follow us inside. Johann watches me make a fuss of them.

On a table is a vase with a deeply luminous black iron glaze. The vase is filled with a great mass of stems with dark purple leaves.

From the big smoke plant by the fence, Johann says, I cut it back before the storm came. That's Dicker pottery.

Johann makes tea. In the front room are some of his new paintings. Big, hand-painted circles in gold-leaf paint on linen. Sometimes the circles are complete, others are open.

I was thrown in the deep end, Johann says as he makes tea, my first day in the walk-in shop in Hastings. I was tattooing a rose on this bloke's arm and Frank, my boss, teacher really, shouted: Hurry up you arty farty wanker, we've got a queue out here!

What was that, twenty-five years ago?

Yeah, and I'm still an arty farty wanker, Johann laughs. When's the book out?

Soon.

We drink the tea. Then Johann stands up.

Right, he says.

Out back of the cottage is a wood-frame building with floor to ceiling windows all around. The wood smells new. We go in. There's a plug-in heater that's been turned on. The room is warm and full of light. Against one wall is a large statue of the Buddha, with offerings of flowers and incense and a wooden bowl of oranges on a low table in front of him. Johann wheels out a folded massage table and sets it up and covers it with sheets of kitchen roll.

I take off my shirt and get on the table.

Johann puts colours into little caps, and fixes them to a paper plate with Vaseline. He puts on surgical gloves, turns on the machine.

When Johann's tattooing me, anger is concentrated in the deep burn and sticking drag of the needles.

Johann wipes my blood away.

He tells me the names of the birds I can see hopping around in the plants and trees outside. He tells me the names of the trees and plants, too.

Gingko, smoke-bush, hawthorn.

When Johann stops tattooing, the anger is gone. I don't know for how long.

You have to find your own solidity.

Johann bins the unused ink, the paper plate, the sheets of bloody kitchen roll, his surgical gloves. He tapes me up, hugs me gently.

How are you really? he says. You see anybody? Steve?

Haven't seen Steve in a while, I say, we fell out.

Well, you want to fall in again, Johann says, and laughs.

Yes.

How are the kids?

All right just now, I say. Jay's writing poetry.

As the bath water turns crimson
and your lips taste of salt
clutching at any single reason not to open
your arm up in search of a sense of peace

Good, says Johann, who's he reading?

There's a bunch of writers he likes I don't know about, I say, but he likes Kerouac.

Johann smiles. The last time I'd seen him he'd come to London to hear me talk about Kerouac.

I've been trying to get him into Whitman, I say.

We'd been in the pub watching Arsenal, and were walking home. Jay had drunk a couple of beers. It's not always easy for him to go to the toilet when he's in a pub. I'd said to him, go just before half-time, but he hadn't. I knew, walking home, that he was desperate to go, so I talked to him about poetry and Whitman. The writers I love, I told Jay, most often write in the first person, in language anybody can understand. It's a good way for people whose lives are considered worthless by the powerful to write their way into existence. Which is most of us. A lot of the stuff I used to like is angry, I said, but more and more I like Whitman. He writes about love.

Unscrew the locks from the doors! I said (I was shouting, I think. Arsenal had won the game right at the end).

> *Unscrew the doors themselves from their jambs!*
> . . .
> *Long enough have you dreamed contemptible dreams,*
> *Now I wash the gum from your eyes,*
> *You must habit yourself to the dazzle of the light*
> *and of every moment of your life.*

All this time Jay had to keep stopping. I didn't think he was listening. Jay squeezed his eyes shut and exhaled hard. He jabbed at his stomach in a gesture I recognized from his childhood, when he often had to be told to go to the toilet. Once, he was doubled over. But I kept talking, and Jay kept breathing out, and we made it home.

In the morning I was worried that I had appeared foolish to my son, or simply drunk. How stupid I'd been to tell Jay to read Whitman. What would he think if he read all that stuff about bathing and Whitman admiring his body?

A few days later, Jay showed me a poem he'd written that began:

> *I celebrate myself,*
> *for my own skin, for the burns on my arms*

for the life I chose to live

and the life I will continue to live

I celebrate myself

This appreciation is a power only you

can bestow upon yourself

So start tomorrow morning

when you look into a mirror and see

this imperfect but perfect being

Leaving the cottage Johann gently punches me. When I look at him he points down at the door, still out of its frame, and laughs.

Herne Hill, London, 2013

There's this other boy, Sunny, who's been coming to the house lately. Sunny's a year or maybe two years younger than Jay.

Do you want a cup of tea? Jay asks him.

No thanks, he says.

Sunny refuses or escapes my attention by looking away or down at the floor. He wants to make himself hard to see. Like a woodland creature, a deer maybe, Sunny's shy for a good reason. I've noticed how he studies Jay though, and I remember how I watched the way Luke did things when we were boys. How my brother moved and spoke. How he held himself in the company of other boys and men. Sometimes I think I've seen Jay watching me the same way.

The tight binder Sunny wears under his grey sweatshirt pushes his chest in. The binders make it hard to breathe. Sometimes if Jay's feeling especially vulnerable he'll wear two at once, knowing that he'll make himself sick, which he'd rather be than found out. Dusty had to practically carry him out of a crowded party once. He looked like a ghost, she told me. I think Jay and Sunny look like they are trying to stand straight against a great pressure. To somebody else – a teacher maybe, a cop – the hunched-over stance, so slight you only wonder about it when they're gone, might make the boys seem suspicious. I've also been guilty of thinking that Jay's sullen because of how he stands, when really he's fighting to breathe, though he can be sullen, too.

Sunny's holding a water bottle filled with some brightly coloured drink, and a big packet of Haribo sweets.

How can you put so much sugar in your tea? he asks Jay.

They have a conversation about sugar. Sunny says that a girl they both know ate twenty packets of sugar at a Costa.

I'm not that bad, Jay says, laughing, his laugh a deep rumble now. I'm trying to cut down. Are you sure you don't want anything?

I'm all right.

I notice how big Jay is next to Sunny, how solid-looking and bulked out. I think too, always, how beautiful he is. Jay's been on testosterone injections for three months. He sometimes uses my weights. There's hair above his lips and on his cheeks.

The dog clips up the stairs with one of Sunny's black and white Vans trainers in her mouth.

The boys think it's hilarious.

Put that back, I say.

The boys go down to Jay's room to talk.

Sacred talk. I imagine them sitting face to face. They are boys but they are also trans boys, and there is always tribal knowledge for Jay to pass on to Sunny. Where did Jay find what he needed? Mostly online, certainly at first, when he hadn't told us and thought he was on his own. Along with his mother's love, it was the internet that saved my son's life. How to pack a sock in your pants so you look like you've got something down there, and your jeans hang right. So that people – boys and men – don't get suspicious, hostile. Jay and Sunny don't need to be told that a fight might only be the start of something worse. Stories about trans boys being raped aren't just stories. Jay knows boys it's happened to, I'm sure. Where do the boys who see Jay and Sunny and smell blood learn to think like that? What's it like to wake up to a world without love?

Sunny's strong. I'm sure of this, I can hear it in his laugh and besides, I know about his life. But he's vulnerable, too. He's so slight, and he's having to go through everything on his own. I am certain that the talks he has with Jay will help save his life, and proud that Sunny loves and trusts my son. Jay has survived so far. Not gone nuts or killed himself like so many trans kids do. The thickest scars on Jay's arms have an ugly shimmer, but they are all old. Who else does Sunny have who'll listen?

I wipe the kitchen counter clean of the sugar Jay spilled, and wash up the teaspoon he used. The dog follows me as I move around. I kiss the dog's nose and scratch her ears.

Poor Sunny, I say to her, but I'm angry, too.

She'd probably love you, I say to the dog. Wouldn't care if you were a boy dog or a girl dog.

The dog looks at me.

You don't care. All you want is a carrot.

She stands up at the word 'carrot', and wags her tail. I take a carrot out of the fridge and break it in two. I give her the bigger piece and she takes it away to her basket by the window.

I hear her slump down and start crunching.

Rose is singing on her way home from school. I can hear her coming down the hill from the bus stop. She bursts in the door, singing, and storms up the stairs. Rose, jet-black dyed hair and red lipstick, lots of piercings. A fake fur coat the same colour as her hair (she's a vegan).

Padre Stein! Rose says.

She hugs me. She smells of smoke. I don't say anything.

Where's Meutre, she says, where's your wife?

Mum's on her course.

Rose kisses the dog.

Hello hound. What have you been eating? Have you been giving her carrots again Dad? Whose shoes are those downstairs?

Sunny's.

Is Sunny here? Oh I love him, he's so adorable!

She clomps downstairs to see Sunny and her brother.

I'm chopping garlic when Rose comes out of Jay's room and back upstairs.

Sunny's aunt is evil, she says.

I don't know that she's evil Rosie.

She's evil Dad.

Sunny must be lonely.

Lucky he's got Jay.

Yes, I say, and you.

I tell the teachers they have to call him Sunny. It shouldn't matter what his aunt says.

What do the teachers say?

That they have to respect what his aunt wants, even though she's an evil cow.

Rose.

What? Do they want to make Sunny crazy?

She carefully chooses an apple from the bowl on the table. Bites into it with a loud crunch so that the dog looks up.

Where are you going now?

Ancient History, she says, with a mouth full of apple. Got to learn the dates of all the battles.

I'll call you when dinner's ready.

OK Padre.

On Sunday I go out walking with my friends Ted and Pat and our dogs. We take a short train ride to Petts Wood. From the station we walk along quiet suburban streets to the woods.

We walk through a culvert under a railway line to get into the wood. The last time we came the culvert was flooded with rainwater and we had to take a long walk round. Though there has been heavy rain, this time we can get through. My dog splashes through the pool of water that remains. The rest of us keep away.

In the woods the dogs run free. Pat's red pit bull – a rescue dog, gentle but highly strung, Ted's blond saluki – a hunting dog from a medieval painting, he's shaped like a fringed star – and my sweet black Lab.

Low sun comes through the trees to us as we walk on

a mud-banked track. I wonder if church architects studied the way light falls in forests.

What do you think Ted?

Ted, gentle, grey dreadlocks past his waist, says, Could be.

He's busy taking photographs, using his long, angular body like a tripod. Ted and I often talk about not having a dad. We've decided it's best to be outside whenever you can.

Steam rises and water drips from the bracken. Through an opening in the canopy of trees I see a jet trail in the sky, a soft white echo of the track we're following. As we pass deeper into the wood more water falls, rain without rain. The dogs chew on wet grass. Ted photographs red rowan berries beaded with dew.

In a meadow we see mating foxes locked together. Are those deer – that sandy movement in the distance? Here's a glade with a brook running through it. A burnt birch tree, hollowed out. Iridescent spider webs in a sunlit patch of wet gorse. The dogs run through the gorse, breaking webs, rolling in wetness. Small clouds of condensation rise in light as wetness dries in sunshine. Was the birch tree hit by lightning?

My dog jumps in the brook and swims in circles. She looks like she's grinning when she climbs the bank and shakes water over us. Downstream shallow water moves over a pebble-bottomed stream. Yellow leaves drift on the surface.

Ted's dog play-attacks my dog because he's jealous of her swimming.

There's this kid, I say, Sunny, he's a mate of Jay's. He lives with his aunt. She still calls him by his birth name. She won't use the name he's chosen.

Ted says, Maybe she's frightened?

Rose says it's because of her religion – doesn't believe there can be any such thing as trans kids. Sunny's a girl to her, that's it.

And there's no Dad, Pat says.

Not here. I think he's back in Nigeria. I don't know how much contact they have.

Pat's from Boston – Boston-Irish. He's the only one of us who knew his dad.

What do you think your dad would have done if you'd told him you were a girl? I ask him. That you were going to live as a girl?

Pat smooths his grey beard.

He wouldn't have heard me, I don't think. I mean he wouldn't have been able to understand what I was saying.

This light, Ted says.

We're deep in the wood, but still the light reaches us.

They've been coppicing, Ted says. Usually when it's light like this there's more cover, so it doesn't reach us in here.

He's right. This is the first spring sunshine we've had, and because of the coppicing there's open light in the wood where for months it's been closed in and dark.

And it wouldn't have been his fault, Pat says. He wouldn't have known any better.

What if your sister told him she was a boy?

Caitlin was a tomboy, Pat says. That's the funny thing.

Every Saturday when my dad went to the barber's she'd go along. Sit in the chair next to him and get her hair cut short like his. But Jesus if Caitlin had told him she was a boy that would have been ten times worse than anything I could have done.

Why? Ted says.

Oh I don't know, Pat says. Just the way men are with their daughters. Pat looks at me. You know that, right? he says.

Back at the house, me and the dog, there's Sunny outside.

Hello mate, I say. Is he not answering?

He's out, he says. With his mum. But he's on his way.

Come in and wait. I open the door. Sunny's still not met my gaze. He doesn't want to. That's all right, although it used to drive me mad when Jay did it.

The dog is sat down on her behind staring at me.

Go on up mate. I've got to get these boots off and feed this dog. Do you want a cup of tea?

No thanks, Jay said he'd be here soon.

I slide open the glass door of the bookcase Robin bought me years ago, and take out *Fires*. It looks, now, like an old book. It's shocking how yellow the pages are. Inside the book is a photo of my daughters at the shoreline. The water – this close in to the shore a kind of sandy foam – is running out behind them and I know they are waiting for the surf to come rushing back in. The kids are really dark, made even darker by the cloud cover you can see above their heads.

Mum took the picture. When Jay and Rose were small

they used to stay with her for a week or sometimes two in the summer, in her light-filled cottage close to the beach in Pevensey Bay, four miles or so east of the beaches where I spent the best part of my boyhood.

Rose stands still, planted, leaning forward, feet pointed outwards for better balance (loving the feeling of wet sand between her toes), knees slightly bent, arms by her side. She is a sturdy, stocky child – she looks just like me at that age – wearing a coral-pink and white bikini. Her fringe covers her eyes and the upper part of her face. You can tell by the smile on her face that she knows she looks sweet and funny because of this and that she's trying to stand still and keep her hair falling across her face and the funny look going. There is a long smear of sun cream on her left bicep that Rose may have put there as a decoration. Mum would have made sure any sun cream she put on her granddaughter was properly rubbed in. The top of Rose's head is almost perfectly in line with the horizon.

Slender, taller, standing slightly behind Rose and pretending to be blown back into the sea by the soft onshore winds you can see gently spuming the shallow water, Jay reaches out to my mum, her left hand shaped like a claw. She wears blue shorts, definitely not bikini bottoms, and no top. Her waist-length hair is all bunched up in back. Mum would have carefully brushed and plaited Jay's hair and coiled it up in a bun. Some of Jay's hair has come loose in front and is waving in ribbons. It's clear from the face she is making, a kind of gritted smile that if you were a kid you would join to a 'grrrr' sound, that Jay is being a monster who wants to get at my mum only the wind won't let her.

Behind my children low incoming breakers make an irregular and broken terrace, shallow lines of illuminated waves shining under the bright vault of the southern sky.

For years I kept the picture of Jay and Rose on the beach at Pevensey Bay with some other favourite photos of my daughters in a big glass frame. In all them – from Mallorca, Accra and Sussex – my girls are suntanned, beautiful, smiling.

Through everything that happened the pictures stayed. In time they became charged with a different meaning. Proof that there had ever been these girls: these sisters Jay and Rose. Then one night Jay – fourteen or so – came home drunk and smashed the glass and ripped the photos from the backing and left the wreckage on the floor for me to find in the morning.

Jay, from a place I couldn't reach, said: It wasn't me Dad. It wasn't me.

The olive paint of the bookcase (the same colour as a dress I bought Robin once) is faded and cracked. The pink flower decoration is almost worn away, and I cannot tell or remember if it was a rose, but I think it was. There are even two cigarette burns, deep ones, on top of the case near the partial flower.

The dog's looking at me. All right, I say, hang on. I bend down to stroke her silky ears.

I'm still holding the book and the photo. I can make out the faint splash of pale freckles on Jay's cheekbone that have always been there and always will be. I put the picture back. Jay will be home soon. I hold the book. It's the title essay, 'Fires', I turn to – and these lines stand from the page: 'Nothing', Carver writes, 'and, brother I mean nothing – that ever happened to me on this earth – could come anywhere close, could possibly be as important to me, could make as much difference, as the fact that I had two children.'

I close the book, and put it back. Gently I slide the glass door shut.

Come on, I say to the dog, let's get you fed, then we'll see about these kids.

Havana, Cuba, 2014

Havana in the early morning is cooler than the southward island we left yesterday, where I'd swum ninety feet down between coral pinnacles shimmering with life and watched my shadow passing over the white sand below. My first dives in the Caribbean, Nick's too. Wild blue. Standing on the stone beach in winter when I was a boy, and watching the rough channel roll and kick up spume, I never dreamed that one day I'd find myself in this shining valley, flying in midday brilliance with phalanxes of barracudas and tarpon bright as tin.

All that's bad in me left behind on the shore. Hoping it will be gone when I return. Shit on the beach washed away by the changing tide.

I've been diving with Nick for over twenty years. From Mombasa we'd searched the Indian Ocean for whale sharks. In the southern Red Sea we had dived for, and found in the endless blue water beyond the reefs, oceanic whitetips and thresher sharks, hammerheads and manta rays. Always these animals were elusive, and if you were lucky enough to come face to face with a flying manta – and I was, one early morning on Daedalus Reef – you could not return from the water unchanged. I dive for this sense of wonder, to hold it close as I return from the blue, rising slowly to light that fractures the water into golden columns.

Cuba was a different voyage. We'd seen no sharks this trip. None of the big stuff.

The Hemingway Marina is deserted.

Carrying our gear, Nick and I walk along the canal-style docks. We haven't returned to Havana to get back in the water, we've other plans for the city, but when Nick asked me if I fancied a last dive out of the Hemingway Marina I couldn't say no.

A squat, flat-roofed white building with blue cornicing has a dive flag – red with a white sash – painted on the wall. Jumping marlins frame the flag. Next to this mural is another painted sign: Centro Buceo – La Aguja. The paintings are worn, abraded by the sun and by neglect. At least the door's open, though from here I can't see if anybody's home.

A frame of rusted white poles projects from the dive shop. The sun is rising behind the building and we stand in shade, as though there really were a canopy above us.

A black and a white man are inside. There's the familiar smell of damp neoprene. The blond white guy has a shark tooth's necklace and a dolphin tattoo. Barefoot, shorts and a vest, Polaroids pushed up in his hair. The black guy – big, with greying, cropped-down hair and big feet – is smoking and sitting on a battered desk. Behind them a window looks out to a sunlit yard, where I can see buoys and ropes, tanks and a portable compressor. A small boat waits at the dockside.

I'd thought there would be more divers but we're the only ones.

We all look at each other for a few seconds. Big Feet suddenly smiles and jumps off the desk and claps his hands.

OK, he says, OK. I'm Bembe, he's Tacito. You ready? Let's go!

We put our kit together out in the yard. Twelve-litre tanks are pumped to 250 bar – it'll be one tank for both dives – and load up the little boat.

Tacito cruises slowly in the canal towards the open water. At the guard house at the end of the canal he shows passes to two boys about Jay's age, wearing khakis that are faded but clean and pressed. Their rifles lean against the sea wall.

The sky is now a pale blue, made paler by the deeper blue of the water that seems directly in my eyeline, we sit so low in the water.

We kit up with no fuss. No wetsuits, just shorts and T-shirts. We backroll over the side. The four of us fly down through the water.

The sea floor is a broken field of bottles and cans, abandoned fishing lines, abstract and rusted engine parts. The reef is dead or dying, the hard corals whited out and shattered. Nick points to sickly-grey brain corals.

It's the harbour after all. But even in this dead landscape there is life. A few yellow butterfly fish are attracted by a ball of bread Bembe carries in his hand. I remind myself I wasn't expecting much. I'm just trying to hold onto this free feeling – flying in this warmth, my dear friend by my side. How's this possible? Above me sunlight illuminates the first few feet of water. We're just hovering here in the blue and the light.

Nick takes about thirty pictures of a small electric ray buried in the sand. The ray finally breaks cover, showering sand everywhere. We stay down for an hour. In the boat, Tacito hands out sandwiches and cold water. The boat rocks gently as we eat. Water slaps at the sides. There's no need to talk. The sun's up now and my T-shirt begins to dry against my skin. The Russian embassy dominates the Havana skyline. Above the buildings the sky is a rose wash.

After the second dive we start back to the Hemingway Marina. It's not the view he'd have had from *Pilar*, of the fortress El Morro and the old town, but even so, I'm coming back to Havana from out on the water just like he did.

The next morning, we go into the city.

From Paseo Che Marti, across the Parque de la Fraternidad to the Ciclo Bus Station.

Crowds line the square, waiting for buses. It's difficult to tell which line is which, until I spot the sign for the 7 bus that goes to San Francisco de Paula, where the house is. We join the line, and wait.

The bus comes. It's crowded, and we stand all the way. People keep asking us to sit down, offering us their seats, but we stand and smile. It's the first time I've been anywhere where most of the people are mixed-race. I ask where to get off, the nearest stop to the house. Everybody knows where it is. By the time we get off the bus I've soaked through my T-shirt.

We're on the main street in San Francisco de Paula. There's a sign for the Finca! We follow it. At the gatehouse a young girl, five or six, sits on the lap of the uniformed guard, flicks the buttons of his shirt, pulls his ear and runs off laughing. The guard smiles after her.

We buy our tickets, and walk up a curving drive lined with hibiscus, royal palms and jacaranda trees into wild gardens canopied with mango trees and bougainvillea vines. The erupted roots of a banyan tree are a massive braided heap near the empty pool. Nearby are the stone and wooden tombs of four of his dogs.

We walk up the steps to the stuccoed, one-floor white house. It's not as big as I imagined. There's nobody else here, on this hot mid-morning, except a member of the museum staff, a young, bright-faced woman, in worn heels, who wants to give us a tour. No, I say, no thank you.

The house is both open and closed. You're not allowed inside.

I look in through open doors and windows that are everywhere, for the light and the cross-breezes they give (nobody to feel the breezes now, or enjoy the light). The centre of each preserved, deserted room is in shade and cool-looking, tropical light pouring in just so far, so that I can almost feel the coolness of the tiles on my bare feet.

I can see him, padding massively in shorts across the floor with a drink in one hand and a book in the other. The whole house suggests his presence by his absence. His slippers by the bed. Wire-framed reading glasses on the night table. Here, in his left behind home, and as he has been all my adult life, he is a dreamed figure, but never before so close.

Dead animal heads dominate each room. Seen through this jellied heat, the kudus and buffaloes – sleek, bright eyed – seem ready to leap down reassembled from the walls in showers of falling masonry and brick dust, and escape to the longed for green and dappled gardens.

Hemingway. When I was young and lived alone in single rooms, the voice in my head that sometimes gave me instruction and which, in a different life, might have been my father's voice, belonged to him.

I'd brought my old copy of *Islands in the Stream* to Cuba – the strange, undisciplined novel published ten years after Hemingway's suicide. It's the only book where he talks about being a father. There's 'Fathers and Sons', but that's really about being a son. Like the best of Hemingway much of the feeling in it is contained: *The towns he lived in were not towns his father knew.*

Islands seemed different. Suddenly here was openness and uncontained feeling. That's what I thought when I first read it as a boy.

Thomas Hudson is a good painter who lives alone in a white house on the island of Bimini in the Gulf Stream. The first part of the book is a story about a summer when his three sons – from two different marriages – come to stay with him. It was a long time before I stopped wanting to be one of those sons, and to have lived a summer like the one in the first part of that book.

The boys are Tom, David and Andrew, the youngest. (Hemingway's three sons were Jack, Patrick and Gregory.) Andrew, Hemingway writes, is a perfect copy of his father, a 'boy born to be quite wicked'. A bad boy who 'was just being good while his badness grew inside him.' Thomas Hudson says they recognized the darkness in each other and knew it was bad. 'They were very close to each other.'

The boys really have four fathers. Thomas Hudson and his friend Roger Davis, a writer who is wasting his talent. Eddy, the rummy cook, and Joseph, the houseboy (described as tall with a very long, very black face. Barefooted, dressed in a white jacket and trousers).

Roger, Tom and David – the 'undersea boy' – go spear-fishing with masks and homemade spears one morning, hunting on the inside of a reef where the wreck of an old steamer shows above the waves. Eddy warns the boys to stay close to Roger and to each other, and to put any fish they catch straight into the dinghy before the blood trails have a chance to spread in the water.

'I can't stand worrying about those kids,' Eddy says, and gets Thomas Hudson to put the boat closer into the reef, and to keep watch with his rifle on the flybridge. Andrew is with Joseph in the dinghy that will stay close to the divers and collect the fish they catch.

When the shark, an enormous hammerhead, comes from the outside ocean and smashes through a hole in the reef, Thomas Hudson knows that he will always remember the height of the shark's fin, the way it wobbles because the shark is moving so fast, and how it turns after David, who has a yellowtail on his spear, 'like a dog on a scent.'

Thomas Hudson fires at the shark, shooting just ahead of the fin and missing each time.

Eddy fires the machine gun: '. . . and the fin went under and there was a boil in the water and the biggest hammerhead he had ever seen rose white-bellied out of the sea and began to plane over the water crazily, on his back, throwing water like an aquaplane. His belly was shining an obscene white, his yard-wide mouth like a turned-up grin, the great horns of his head with the eyes on the end, spread wide out as he bounced and slid over the water, Eddy's gun rapping and ripping into the white of his belly making black spots that were red before he turned and went down and Thomas Hudson could see him rolling over and over as he sank.'

I had seen dead sharks in Mexico, heaped in the back of a flat-bed truck near the beach at Estacahuite on the Pacific coast, looking too small and dully lead-coloured, but those live hammerheads I had been lucky enough to see, moving in slow undulations in the deep blue waters of the Red Sea, were not ugly, the way Hemingway writes his shark, but so beautiful that when I finally saw the first I yelled happily to Nick through my regulator, and made a backwards somer-sault in the water, my body's perfect circle ringed by a silver loop of my exultant breath.

Patrick Hemingway said that *Islands* was based on a trip that he and Gregory took with their father, 'the last really great, good time we all had together', just before the war. It was, he said, 'my last real happy memory of childhood.' He also said: 'no one was ever attacked by a shark.'

In his memoir *Papa*, Gregory Hemingway writes that there *was* a shark attack. He says he was spearfishing (strangely he calls it scuba diving) and was in the water with his father. There's no mention of Patrick. Gregory is alone in the water with his father.

Three huge sharks, 'each more than eighteen foot long', come towards Gregory in 'slow S-shaped curves.' The boy has stored the fish he's caught, looping his belt through their gills, and of course the sharks are attracted by the blood scent that has travelled in the water. Gregory screams uncontrollably.

'Even over the sound of the waves, my father could hear me.'

Gregory swims to Hemingway, who puts the boy on his shoulders and swims to the dinghy and safety.

'I never felt more like his son than I did that day,' Gregory writes.

Gregory says that this 'real incident' became the scene about 'a shark attacking my brother in *Islands in the Stream*.'

The sharks are too big, I think, and there are too many of them. How could the terrified boy in the water know the size of the sharks? Poor, brilliant, tormented Gregory – Gigi – who exaggerated and lied. Why does he have to be alone in the water with his father? So much in *Papa* is untrustworthy or not said, but this does not make it any less of a true story. What's really being said is buried at least as deeply as it is in his father's books.

When I first read *Islands* I knew nothing about Hemingway's youngest son, the model for the bad and wicked Andrew. What made him bad and wicked?

In 1951, when he was nineteen, married and soon to be a father, Gregory was arrested in an LA movie house women's toilet, dressed as a woman.

On Sunday, 30 September 1951, Gregory's mother Pauline Pfeiffer rings Ernest to tell him that his son has been arrested and why. That Gigi's wickedness and badness had become public. The parents fight. Perhaps Ernest blames his ex-wife for his son's actions. Pauline goes to bed, but wakes just after midnight with severe abdominal pains. She's taken to hospital, where doctors discover and try to stop the internal bleeding. Pauline's blood pressure falls. She dies of shock on the operating table at 3 a.m.

In *Papa*, Gregory doesn't tell the truth about why he was arrested, only that he 'got into some trouble on the West Coast for taking a mind-stimulating drug before such things had become fashionable.' His father blamed Gregory for Pauline's death. Called him 'harbour scum'.

Why do Thomas and Andrew Hudson recognize the darkness in each other?

In Hemingway's *The Garden of Eden*, another novel published after his suicide, David and Catherine Bourne are honeymooning in southern France. The newlyweds look alike, especially after Catherine has her bleached-blonde hair cut short as a boy's. In bed after Catherine has cut her hair, David 'lay there and felt something and then her hand holding him and searching lower and he helped with his hands and then lay back in the dark and did not think at all and only felt the weight and the strangeness inside and she said, "Now you can't tell who is who can you?"

"No."

"You are changing," she said. "Oh you are. You are. Yes you are and you're my girl Catherine." '

—

In late September 2001, aged sixty-nine, Gregory (or Gloria, or Vanessa sometimes) was arrested in Florida, naked except for a hospital gown around his shoulders, holding a red jumper and black high heels. He had one breast implant. His genitalia had been surgically altered – Gigi had labia and a vagina. His toenails were painted red. 'I've spent hundreds of thousands of dollars,' he once said, 'trying not to be a transvestite.' Which could mean many things, but one possible meaning is that the surgery he bought was intended to help him become the woman he believed himself to be (or not, Gigi was married several times and had many children).

On Monday, 1 October 2001, Gigi collapsed and died in pod 377 of the third-floor cellblock of the Miami-Dade women's detention centre.

Even over the sound of the waves, my father could hear me.

We sit on the cool steps with our backs to Hemingway's house.

You remember the hammerheads we saw on Daedalus Reef? I say to Nick.

(*You never saw such wonderful reefs*, Thomas Hudson says about the Red Sea.)

Course, why?

You wouldn't want one stuffed and mounted down in Walthamstow?

No, he laughs, different times though.

Yes mate, I hope so.

If we'd been around in the early days, he says, I reckon we'd have thought differently, probably done some spearfishing. Thought the only good shark was a dead shark.

Maybe. Did you spearfish when you were a kid in Cyprus?

No, never felt like it.

There you go then.

Nick's silent for a bit.

We never finished the diving course with the kids, I say.

He looks at me. You had a lot on your plate, he says.

Maybe, I say, but I should have found a way.

Hemingway. I can't ignore it any longer. Those death heads on every wall. What drives the slaughter? When Gregory believed he was responsible for his mother's death because of the 1951 arrest, he went to Africa with his inheritance – blood money, he called it: 'I shot eighteen elephants one month, God save my soul.'

What I really wanted to be, Gigi wrote, was a Hemingway hero. A son of a bitch, in Gregory's words, who was also full of love and empathy and understanding. A man who loved him and called him harbour scum. Would I have accepted the damage that came with being his son, to have been able to say this:

Even over the sound of the waves my father could hear me.

Once I would have. There was a time I'd have done anything, hidden away any part of myself my father didn't like (with no guarantee he'd hear me, even then).

Of the infinite things he might have thought about, did Hemingway think about his children in the moments before he took down the shotgun and silenced for ever all the voices in his head? Suicide, Thomas Hudson says, would be a hell of an example for the boys.

Nick's watching me. I look at him. I know he'll wait here for as long as I need. I look at the thick sun cream covering his fair face and forearms. I remember that Nick doesn't like the sun. I stand up, dust myself down.

Don't be so hard on yourself, Nick says.

Herne Hill, London, 2014

Jay says he's going to Australia.

Australia!

Australia's a long way away, although to my son it might seem like no distance at all.

Jay's eighteen. He's saved money (from his weekend job in a bookshop) and he's been given money and soon he will fly out. He'll be gone for six weeks. He's never been away from us before.

Australia is not a place Araba's ever wanted to visit (I'd love to go, for the chance to dive with whale sharks at Ningaloo Reef, especially). My wife keeps a large lithograph print of a black woman standing in a bright coastal landscape (the sand is yellow, the sea is blue) above the words: You are on aboriginal land.

Australia, Araba says. No. It wouldn't be the same country for me as it would for you.

I don't argue with her. In Rome some men who saw us walking together called her a prostitute because she was black and with me. I saw Araba hesitate, and take a half-step before continuing, but I did not understand until she told me later what the men had said. She did not cry. Her face was fierce.

I've been expecting it, she said. It's still what happens.

Prosperous-looking young men in sunglasses, wearing

pastel-coloured jumpers around their shoulders, drinking coffee at an outside table of a smart-looking restaurant near the Via Verri. The table cluttered with slim phones and keys to the shining cars parked high on the pavement so that we could not walk together, but only in single file, with Araba, lovely, dark in a blue summer dress patterned with yellow flowers, her back straight, her hair pulled away from her long neck, walking ahead.

Nera puttana.

Black whore.

I told myself there had been too many of them, but I felt unmanned.

Despite what she thinks about the place, Araba is really positive about Jay going to Australia.

It's me who's worried, at least out loud. It isn't so long ago that Jay was mugged. Not just for his phone and money, but for who he is. Maybe the boys who attacked Jay were just looking for money. But why did they need to beat him? Why did they call him a dyke, and say they were going to rape him?

There were too many of them. Jay wasn't tough enough to fight them all. (But I think, too, that he believed I'd be disappointed in him for not being tough.) My son's tears would not stop.

Was he thinking, Do I have to be this kind of boy to survive? Is this what being a boy is?

I dream of killing the men who called my wife a whore because she's black. I want to find and beat the boys who hurt my son because they could. What stops me is knowing that the violence would not be for Araba and Jay. I thought that I was not that kind of man any more, but it's always in me.

It's hard not to hate, I tell Jay. Yourself or other people. You have to try not to give in to it. Meanwhile are there any trans self-defence classes?

I email my friend Geo in Melbourne – Jay's going to Melbourne – to get his contact details and give him Jay's email address. In case there's an emergency, I want Jay to have somewhere to go. Geo's a poet. He's Greek, too, like Jay. Mostly I'd say Jay looks Greek. But he doesn't like the sun, because wearing binders makes it hard for him to breathe, and the heat makes it harder. So he's pale, and it's hard to see him as African. He's going to Australia and he doesn't like the sun.

Geo tells me about the anti-Greek violence out there – he doesn't need to mention the transphobia because it's a given. The anti-Greek stuff is something else for me to worry about. Geo says he'll find out where the transgender support group is located. There's also a poetry reading in Sydney – maybe Jay would like to come with him, take a road trip just like the ones Geo has taken with his old man, to Texas and California, and to Jack Kerouac's home town of Lowell, Massachusetts, where Geo and I stood by Kerouac's grave and cried when we read what it said there: *Ti Jean. John L. Kerouac. He Honored Life.*

All my worries go flying over Jay's head.

All he cares about is that he's finally going to meet Carmelita.

For a long time after he was mugged Jay stayed in his room. This was now his life – he'd be a victim for ever. Who would feel any differently? His attackers had taken away the thing he was still searching for. His manhood. Then he met Carmelita online. She's the first girl he's been interested in since Dusty.

Carmelita's a beauty. I've waved at the screen to say hello to her. She's Maltese, Maltese-Australian. Jet-black hair and huge black eyes. A doll. She's always in bed when I wave hello at her, her pretty face peeking out from the covers. Sometimes I think she looks a bit like Jay might have looked if he hadn't been a boy. He's crazy in love with her and I can't blame him. He can't wait to meet her. I'm sure he dreams of holding her in his arms.

Now it's Carmelita who talks to him through the night and stops him cutting himself or worse.

I shame myself and these children by wondering how their relationship can work and survive.

Until Australia, he's mostly here. Downstairs in his room, Skyping Carmelita for hours, sleeping or not sleeping, writing secret poems. Dreaming about his unwritten future.

But not, as far as I can tell, cutting himself any more.

What if some beered-up bunch of Australian men see Jay and Carmelita together, and decide she shouldn't be with my son?

I will not be there to help him.

What if it doesn't work out when he and Carmelita finally meet? What if he can't stay there. What's he going to do then?

Why are you so negative? he says.

Araba says it too: Jay says you're really down on him about this trip.

I'm not being negative, I say.

Don't worry, Geo writes, he can come here any time. For some food or a change of clothes or just some space.

I ask Jay if he's emailed Geo to thank him and say hello.

No, Jay says.

You need to write to him, I tell Jay. Even if you end up not seeing him you need to write to him. He's my friend.

All right Dad!

I'm going to see Carmelita, he tells his mum, why would I want to hang out with Dad's friends? Don't I realize he and Carmelita have been talking for months, for hours every day? They're in love, there aren't going to be any problems.

When I write to Geo to tell him that Jay probably won't be getting in touch, and to say sorry because I know Geo will have been looking forward to meeting my son, and gone to a lot of trouble to find out the things Jay might need, Geo says: Hey, don't worry, I understand, he wants to be with his friends. You remember what it's like being that age.

Jay's a poet, I say to Araba. I thought he'd want to meet Geo.

Lots of Jay's friends are poets too, she says.

I can't believe how calm Araba is being about this. Jay's never been anywhere on his own before. Nobody knows him as well as his mother though, that's true.

—

Downstairs, I hear Jay opening his door.

His bedroom door has never sat properly in its frame. I'm no carpenter but I've planed the door so that it does not stick as badly as it used to. But it still does stick, and when Jay opens his door I hear it. I wish that I was a carpenter so that I could show my son how to be one, too. Then I could show Jay what I know and help him that way. Or just so I could fix it myself – my son's door – and not need another man to do it for me.

Again I remember the Gary Snyder poem, 'Axe Handles'. Snyder showing his son, Kai, how to throw an axe. Something I'll never do!

I am an axe, Snyder writes, and my son is a handle, soon to be shaping again.

Hi Dad.

Here's Jay.

He's grown again!

I have to admit he's as tall as me, which means he's six feet.

He gives me a cheesy grin, then puts his arms high above his head, keeping his hands loose. He bends his knees and starts sliding backwards and forwards across the wooden floor, waving one arm up and down and then the other.

Orangutan, I say.

Jay collapses laughing and goes to hug the dog in her basket by the window.

Jay's almost black hair is cut in a new, going-to-Australia flattop – a smart quiff and shaved at the back and sides (he goes to the same barber's I first took him to, but he goes on his own now). He wears black-framed glasses and a nose ring – he says the nose ring stops people thinking about his girly face. He's not wearing a binder under his T-shirt. It is a sure sign he's feeling good if he's able to go without his binder in the house.

He hugs me as I sit at the table. He smells stale and dirty. He wants to make himself some food. I know I need to find somewhere else to work, that it's selfish, but I like to write at the kitchen table in this house that sits high on a hill, and where all morning the light comes in from the south. The sky here is high and blue. The view down past the silver birch trees that line the road directly in front of the house takes in the city.

I've never found a better place to work. It's so quiet here.

I put down my pen.

How are you Dadda? Jay says.

I'm good, I say, wishing he would go away.

I haven't got time to make you lunch, I think. I'm working. Make your own lunch. You don't do anything all day. He moves around behind me. Boils the kettle for tea. Puts in at least four sugars. Gets a bowl and fills it with cornflakes. He doesn't eat properly unless somebody makes the food for him.

It's nearly lunchtime, I say, and you're just having breakfast.

I've been up for hours Dad, he says.

Which may or may not be true. I know that often he doesn't come up here because he knows I'm working. Either because he understands I need quiet to work, or because he doesn't want me to have a go at him. So why am I having a go at him? What does it mean that I don't want him around when I'm trying to make him up – to make him real to people who don't know him, who won't know whether I got him right or not?

I'm thinking too much. I have to allow for it to be normal for my teenage son to madden me – to be messy and dirty and sleep late and eat nothing but pasta and cereal.

Araba never forgets Jay is always passing – which means she never forgets how permanently vulnerable he is, but I do. Does this mean I don't think about him enough? I don't know, but I know that a lot of the time when I'm pissed off with my son, it's because I'm only seeing him as my *son*.

Less than a week now, I say.

Jay's gently teasing the dog – he loves the dog we bought for him but never walks her (because he feels exposed when he goes outside, or because he's lazy?). He's trying to get her ears to stand on end. He's blowing on her muzzle to get her to snap at him.

I'm very excited, he says.

I don't want to say anything. I want to let him be excited.

What happens if things go wrong out there, I say. You can't just turn round and come home.

Dad, nothing will go wrong, he says.

Leave the dog alone.

Fine, he says, clearly pissed off that his dad's still a grumpy dick, but too excited about Australia and Carmelita to worry about it for long.

I'm going to have a bath, he says.

Good, I say, because you stink.

I know that he knows I'm going to say this. He laughs.

As soon as he's gone and I've got what I want, I want to call him back and say sorry. I want to tell him I love him. I'll go to him soon and he'll forgive me.

Jay comes down the stairs, wrapped in a big white towel. His glasses are steamed up and I know he's done this deliberately to make me laugh. He's smiling.

I think about Jay in the bath. When he can't avoid the difference between what he is on the inside and the outside. When he was a little kid, but after Jay and Rose had stopped taking baths together, he used to take his Game Boy up there, hidden in a towel, and sit on the side of the bath. He just hated taking a bath, but I'm not sure back then that he knew why.

He hates his body so much. He has no control over it. He has trained himself not to look down at his body. These are some of the things he tells us.

How can I be surprised that he cuts himself?

Now, when he does get in the bath, he stays in for a long time. Hours. I worry about what he does in there. That I'll have to break the door down and find him unconscious or worse in a bath of bloody water.

So yes, Australia.

I'm going to get dressed, he says.

He comes upstairs again to check the bus times on my laptop. He looks great. Black quiff, black glasses, black T-shirt and jeans. Black leather jacket. A beautiful boy.

You look great, I say. Very cool.

He beams at me.

OK Dad, see you later, he says, I love you.

I love you too.

He clomps downstairs. More faffing about in the downstairs bathroom. Finally he leaves the house, calling out what he always does:

OK, I'm off, I've got my phone, I've got my keys.

And out he goes.

Where the boys and men are who want to do him harm. Boys like the ones who beat him. Men like the ones who called his lovely mother a black whore. But other men too, like Geo, and Nick and Johann. Like Ponyboy Curtis and Jack Kerouac and Walt Whitman. Like all the friends and books and paintings and music he has discovered and will discover for himself, and that he will pass on to the children he will surely have. There is so much love in him. Carmelita's out there, and Australia (and he won't want to hear this now, because his love for Carmelita is true, but other girls in other countries).

And thousands of kids like Jay who will live, becoming fully and at last themselves, while in the becoming they will fully be themselves too, just like all of us.

I watch him from the window. He lights a cigarette, a roll-up – all the kids smoke roll-ups these days – sets his shoulders, and walks out of my sight and into the world.

And I have to let him go.

Herne Hill, London, 2015

Jason's here at last. What will I say to him, now he's at my door with the lowering sun flaring behind him so that it's difficult for me to see his face, and yet I know it's him? I've been locked in too long. I won't allow it any longer. Lately I've begun to think about my father as a man coming invited to the garden where on warm nights my friends and I often meet to tell stories.

Come in, I say, come in. Let me take that.

Jason steps into my house.

We're out here, I say.

By the garden door is Robin's bookcase. I've filled it with books I love. It stands now against walls I've painted, on a wood floor I have swept.

Jason and I come out to the garden, where perfumed flowers are bright constellated signs of love and attention. He rubs his face, searches in his suit pockets for a lighter, lights his cigarette. Takes a big gulp of wine and reaches for the bottle. I think he might have had a drink before he came here. Maybe he's nervous.

I roll my own cigarette, study his face in the falling light. I really do look like him. It's a face dominated by his eyes – not especially large or dark or wide, but in their expressiveness seemingly all these things. Araba says she can tell by my eyes what I'm feeling. When I look at Jason I see what she means. We have the same dark eyebrows, the same thick lips that Araba loves to kiss. (Rose is the same. My daughter looks like us.) We are nearly the same age. We look like brothers.

This is a nice place.

Do you like the garden?

Yes.

Look at the flowers Araba and I have grown together.

In winter and the early spring I help my wife plant seeds that months later flower in lovely surprise. Now, on this soft May evening, the sun falling, here are wine-red peonies in lush brilliance. Yellow soldier's buttons. Tall, creamy dog-daisies. Bluebells, comfrey, wild garlic. Almost transparent orange poppies. Three rose trees in bud by the fence.

My friends are here.

Happy, I let them in. There is a burst of noise and laughter. They come out into the garden.

Jason looks up.

Don't drink too much, I think. Don't get angry and show yourself up in front of these men. But if you do they'll forgive you.

Johann's staying the night, before going back to Sussex, where he has a new wife and daughter.

What have you got there? I say.

Poems and wine, Johann says.

Ted's radiant, grey-blue eyes make his gaunt face gentle and soft despite its being all angles – a big-nosed, long face, framed by a snowy beard and waist-length grey-white dreadlocks – it's the face of a happy goat. He wears a corduroy jacket with a sheepskin lining, canvas work trousers, work boots. Ted's just back from a month trekking in India.

Jay and Carmelita looked after his place while he was away. I was upset that they forgot to water Ted's garden. Ted said – It's OK, it just reminded me what it's like to be nineteen.

Jay left this at mine, he says, and hands me my battered copy of *Leaves of Grass*.

Thanks, I say, I've been wondering where that got to.

Nick and Ted are helping me make a space at the back of the garden to work in. I have pulled up the weeds and started levelling off the ground. This house stands on an old bomb site. Every time Araba or I dig into the ground we find buried debris from the old house. Nick's going to measure up the ground, and work out what materials I'll need for the footings.

We could have done this in the daytime but it's an excuse to drink wine in the garden for the first time this year.

You'll need a tonne of ballast, Nick says, reading from a list he's written on a brown paper bag, six bags of cement, a roll of polythene damp-proof coursing, an insulation sheet, 6 by 2 timber – get them sawn into 2 × 3 metre lengths and 2 × 2 metre lengths – a 2 metre length of 4 by 2 timber to level off the concrete, a box of red wine, music to stop me getting bored and going home and a few women who like middle-aged builders.

Right, I say, laughing. Is that all?

If I think of anything else I'll let you know, he says, putting his glasses back into his shirt pocket.

Meanwhile Ted is going to help me dig up and transport a large, almost twelve-foot-high olive tree that has come to dominate the garden. The dark twisting branches are blocking out the light. I've exposed the roots.

It'll be good for everyone when you have a place to work, Johann says.

Be a while until I get the money.

That's all right, Ted says. We'll get rid of the obstacles. You can sit out here and look at where it's going to go.

If you wait till I've got a vehicle again, Nick says, we can knock up with a mixer and save ourselves a heart attack and the NHS a load of money.

I bring more wine down from the kitchen. The dog follows me up and down the open-plan stairs. When she comes down she runs ahead of me and jumps onto my seat (an old sunbed like the one Mum used to have in her garden).

Hey, I say, shift up.

I sit next to the dog, and kiss her on the nose. I fill my friends' glasses and then I look inside the book of poems Johann's given me (by Olson, Wieners, Ginsberg and others). I find an old favourite. A poem I first read long ago, when words hit like electric shocks:

We're not our skin of grime, we're not dread bleak dusty imageless locomotives, we're golden sunflowers inside

I drink wine. It's warm out here. Summer's not far away.

Johann is looking through the garden door at Robin's bookcase. Inside is a photo of Mum when she was a suntanned girl (dear, unknowable) in a white dress and sandals, with her ragged, grinning mongrel dog, Rex, their shadows clearly printed on sunlit ground, and another of Luke and me when we were little kids, sitting in the bright softness of a meadow filled with buttercups and daisies.

That's not a first edition of *Junky*? Johann says.

No mate, no such luck. We'd be drinking better wine if it was. It's a nice copy though.

Ted draws out and waves a huge imaginary knife: I'm not expecting any trouble, he drawls. A fantastic Burroughs impression.

After we stop laughing I say, I was reading his last journals.

Who, Burroughs? Johann says.

Yeah, you know what the last entry says? Just before he died?

You've told us before but I can't remember, Nick says.

More laughing.

Something about love, Johann says.

Burroughs wrote: Love? What is it? Most natural painkiller what there is. LOVE.

The same Burroughs who killed his wife and ruined his son's life? Johann says.

I know, I say, I know, was it too late?

There is a shining moon. The night sky is a high bright vault. There are even stars. The fronds of a palm tree – from next door's garden – are floating shadows on the fence.

—

I've forgotten about Jason. He's gone. I want to call him back. There were things I wanted to say, to ask him.

It's mattered too much that you never lifted me up, or called me son.

Did you dream about us? About me? You must have missed Luke.

You're not a monster. And you would have wondered about me. Been sorry.

She was so young. How did you think she was going to survive? She did though. The best of me is her.

I'm sorry you were so scared.

Maybe you thought you had no choice but I can't understand how you could go without seeing me.

Dad, stop crying.

Your daughter loved you, your youngest son, too.

You caused a lot of unhappiness, it's true. I know what that's like. But I have carried my children on my shoulders. I've felt their arms around me.

Dad, I'd say, reaching out to touch him, you have to forgive yourself.

My mum, Gillian Cunnell, died on October 19th, 2016, just before this book went to press. My brother and I were with her when she died. Among her neatly kept papers I found her marriage certificate. My mother was seventeen when she married my father – she would not be eighteen for another ten days. My father was eighteen. I also found mum's divorce certificate, dated 8th February 1968. The grounds given for granting the divorce were that my father had 'deserted the petitioner without cause.'

There was also a letter to my mother from one of my father's relatives. The letter is dated 20 August 1996, and reads in part as follows: 'I am sorry to tell you that Jason died of cancer of the liver on 29 July 1996 at the Royal Marsden Hospital, Sutton. I went to his funeral service which was on Tuesday 6 August at 2.30 at Guildford Crematorium and was very well attended – he was obviously very popular – his ashes will be scattered somewhere in the country over the hills.'

My mum's funeral service took place on Tuesday 1st November, at Eastbourne Crematorium, at half past two in the afternoon.

Acknowledgements

Names have been changed.

I am deeply grateful for Paul Baggaley's faith, encouragement and help. This book would not exist without his friendship.

Conversations with Nigel Gilderson, Ted Giles, Angus MacLennan, Bradley Richards and Pete Sutherland opened up the spaces in my head where this book was written.

Thanks to Kester Aspden, Austin Collings, Matthew Loukes, Jim MacAirt, Chris Salewicz, Duncan White and Naomi Wood for reading the book as it developed, and for their helpful criticism. Once again Kris Doyle's editorial work and careful attention have been invaluable.

Pages 139–147 were first published, in slightly different form, as the story 'Transoceanic', in *Litro*, August 2015.

The author acknowledges his debt to the following works:

Biyi Bandele, *Death Catches the Hunter* (Amber Lane Press, 1995)

William S. Burroughs, *Last Words: The Final Journals of William S. Burroughs* (Grove Press, 2000)

Raymond Carver, 'Alcohol; Fires' (from *Fires* by Raymond Carver. Published by Harvill Press. Reprinted by permission of The Random House Group Limited.)

Allen Ginsberg, 'Sunflower Sutra' (from *Selected Poems 1947–1995*, Penguin, 1997)

Ernest Hemingway, 'Fathers and Sons' (from *The Nick Adams Stories*, Scribners, 1972); *Islands in the Stream* (Collins, 1970); *The Garden of Eden* (Hamish Hamilton, 1986)

Gregory Hemingway, *Papa: A Personal Memoir* (Houghton Mifflin, 1976)

Patrick Hemingway, 'Islands in the Stream: A Son Remembers' (in *Ernest Hemingway: The Writer in Context*, edited by James Nagel, The University of Wisconsin Press, 1984)

S. E. Hinton, *The Outsiders* (Viking, 1967)

Jack Kerouac, *Mexico City Blues* (Grove Press, 1959: thanks to John Sampas, Literary Representative of the Estate of Jack Kerouac); *The Subterraneans* (Andre Deutsch, 1960)

Gary Snyder, 'Axe Handles' (from *Axe Handles*, North Point Press, 1983)

Walt Whitman, 'Leaves of Grass' (from *Leaves of Grass, The First (1855) Edition*, edited by Malcolm Cowley, Penguin, 1976)

For the details of Gregory Hemingway's life and death I am indebted to Paul Hendrickson's definitive and indispensable *Hemingway's Boat: Everything He Loved in Life, and Lost, 1934–1961* (The Bodley Head, 2012).

Like everything else, this book is for Adjoa.